THE LEADER'S SUITCASE

Essential Equipment for the Leader's Journey

Setting Yourself Up for Success

Carolyn Stuart

Copyright © 2023 Carolyn Stuart
All rights reserved.

All rights reserved. No part of this publication may be reproduced, distributed, or transmitted in any form or by any means, including photocopying, recording, or other electronic or mechanical methods, without the prior written permission of the publisher, except in the case of brief quotations embodied in critical reviews and certain other noncommercial uses permitted by copyright law.

Every effort has been made to trace and seek permission for the use of the original source material used within this book. Where the attempt has been unsuccessful, the publisher would be pleased to hear from the author/publisher to rectify any omission.

First published in 2023 by Hambone Publishing
Melbourne, Australia

Cover Design by Mike Burrows
Editing by Mish Phillips, Laura McCall and Felicity Harrison
Typesetting and Design by David W. Edelstein

For information about this title, contact:
Carolyn Stuart
carolyn@carolynstuart.com
https://carolynstuart.com

ISBN 978-1-922357-60-1 (paperback)
ISBN 978-1-922357-61-8 (eBook)

Praise for The Leader's Suitcase

The Leader's Suitcase uniquely blends Carolyn's considerable leadership experience with positive psychology concepts to offer insights for aspiring and experienced leaders.

    Dr Julie Mackey - Associate Professor University of Canterbury

I love how it weaves research and Carolyn's own experience and wisdom about leadership into highly practical strategies.

    Sarah Martin - Principal Stonefields School

Carolyn takes us on a journey that develops our self-awareness as leaders and moves us from survival mode to thriving as leaders.

    Neil Heyward - Principal Riccarton High School

The Leader's Suitcase shows us that aspirational leadership is something we can attain and it shows the 'why', the 'how' and the 'what'!

    Joanne Orr - Across-School Lead

Carolyn has created the perfect mix of research, personal stories and strategies to engage us, whatever stage of your leadership story.

    Karen Stewart - Former Principal Rangiora High School

A refreshing read, and a book that will surely be in the reference section for many a leadership institution in our brave new world.

    Dynes McConnell - Women's Health Surgeon

The Leader's Suitcase is my 'go-to' leadership book. I love the balance of key ideas, stories and practical tools.

    Dr Judy Bruce - Education Consultant and Researcher

Carolyn's work offers us an insight into ourselves as leaders, welcoming us on a journey of exploration.

    Lucy Tomlinson - Deputy Principal Pakuranga College

As I read The Leader's Suitcase *I found I kept nodding and saying "Yes." The content is relatable and readable.*

    Andrew Murray - Principal St Mary's College, Wellington

To my amazing husband, Geoff.

*Your unwavering support, love and faith have
enabled me to pursue my passion for the work I do.*

*Thank you for managing all the background logistics,
to give me the space to write.*

Contents

Preface..xiii

Foreword..xvii

Introduction...xix

1. Becoming a Positive Deviant............................. 3
   Survival Mode.. 7
   Thriving Not Surviving.............................. 13
   From Surviving to Thriving.......................... 15
   Chapter Summary..................................... 18
   From Ideas to Action................................ 19

2. Meaning.. 21
   Purpose... 24
   Coherence... 29
   Significance.. 30
   The Hero's Journey.................................. 31
   Chapter Summary..................................... 36
   From Ideas to Action................................ 37

3. Personal Values.. 39
   Personal Values..................................... 41
   Making Explicit the Things that Matter.............. 43
   Identity as a Leader................................ 48
   Chapter Summary..................................... 53
   From Ideas to Action................................ 54

4. Decisions, Boundaries, and Habits...................... 55
   Decisions... 56
   Boundaries.. 60

Habits 66
Chapter Summary. 70
From Ideas to Action 71

5. Strategies for Success 73
Working from Strengths 77
Happiness and Positive Emotions 77
Time and Workload Management 78
Positive Change and Positive Goals 78
Positive Deviance and False Positivity 79
Chapter Summary. 81
From Ideas to Action 82

6. Working from Strengths 83
Aware 85
Explore 86
Apply 87
Chapter Summary. 93
From Ideas to Action 94

7. Happiness and Positive Emotions 95
Happiness 96
Being Happy is Important 99
Eudaimonic and Hedonic Happiness 100
Positive Emotions 103
Gratitude, Savouring and Optimism 106
Amplifying the Impact of Positive Emotions 107
Chapter Summary. 110
From Ideas to Action 111

8. Time and Workload Management 113
Time Management 114
Valuing Your Time 116
Task-Switching 118
Making the Best Use of Your Time 120

>   *Workload Management* *122*
>   *Chapter Summary*....................................... *126*
>   *From Ideas to Action* *127*

9. Positive Change and Positive Goals **129**
>   *Positive Change* *131*
>   *Positive Goals*.. *136*
>   *Chapter Summary*....................................... *142*
>   *From Ideas to Action* *143*

10. Packed and Ready..**145**
>   *Inner Circle*.. *146*
>   *Second Circle* *147*
>   *Third Circle*.. *148*
>   *Ready Set Go*.. *152*

Packing Cell Two: Setting Others Up for Success 153

Packing Cell Three: Setting Organisations Up for Success.....155

References..157

Praise for *The Leader's Suitcase*............................163

About the Author 167

Mā te huruhuru ka rere te manu.

Adorn the bird with feathers so that it may soar.

Preface

I have always been fascinated by leadership, so I guess it was inevitable that if I was ever to write a book it would be about leadership. This started as one book, but I quickly realised that I had too much to say to fit within one tome. I wanted to write books that busy leaders enjoyed picking up and reading and that were arranged in a way that made it easy to locate the tools and strategies needed at any given moment.

The idea for The Leader's Suitcase Trilogy came from thinking about leadership as a journey. As I reflected on my leadership journey, I remembered all the times another leader shared a piece of their knowledge with me, equipping me to be a better leader. I was always grateful for leadership advice that came from another's experience, and that set me up for success ahead of time.

When I travel I like to be well-equipped and prepared for every eventuality. I carry with me a well-organised suitcase that contains just the things I need and nothing more. I'm a great fan of packing cells as they make it easy to quickly locate what I need. Thinking about my physical packing cells, which enable me to quickly find what I need when I need it, is where I got the idea to organise The Leader's Suitcase into three packing cells:

- Setting Yourself Up for Success
- Setting Others Up for Success
- Setting Organisations Up for Success

This book is the first packing cell, Setting Yourself Up for Success. It weaves together insights from the field of Positive Psychology with leadership strategies. I had just started studying my Diploma in Positive Psychology when my mother unexpectedly died. The shock of her death caused my father, who was in the early stages of dementia, to go into a rapid cognitive decline from which he never recovered.

As I navigated this very difficult period of my life I realised how much the positive psychology strategies I was learning about were helping. I then began to wonder what impact the deliberate application of positive psychology might have on leaders. As I began to write about this in my weekly blog the idea of being a positive deviant, someone who deviated from the norm - but in a positive way seemed to really resonate. Leaders loved the idea of thriving instead of just surviving.

This book in no way takes the place of the formal study of positive psychology. My aim in writing it is to make the benefits of positive psychology accessible to leaders who do not have the time to do their own formal study. I hope that as leaders read this book and apply the tools and strategies to both their personal and professional lives, they will flourish.

Nowadays, I spend most of my time working with leaders. I run Masterclasses based on my writing and facilitate workshops with leaders and their teams to design strategies that take them to the next stage of their journey. I also speak at conferences. The leaders I work with tell me how much they appreciate me showing up with ideas, strategies and stories that they can use on their leadership journey. I see my work as equipping leaders for success.

Carolyn

Foreword
by Dr Rosemary Barnett

In *The Leader's Suitcase*, author Carolyn Stuart describes leadership as a journey in which it is important to carry a well-equipped and organized suitcase. The different packing cells within the suitcase contain specific items for different leadership purposes or activities.

With a purposefully, well-packed suitcase, leaders can thrive on their journey and not just "survive" it. When thriving, leaders ensure their own success and can become the leaders they aspire to be, significantly contributing to the success of others and of the organisations that they lead.

With a passion to help equip others to be successful, Carolyn Stuart draws on her life experience in leadership roles as a teacher and then school principal for many years before becoming a senior leader in a company delivering important digital technology to NZ schools. She also draws on extensive recent psychology research, her own design thinking and leadership practice and her training in the field of Positive Psychology to challenge the reader to become a "positive deviant".

By using meaning to underpin the "why" of leadership, by understanding their values to build an identity as a leader and by taking action which is congruent with these values, a "positive deviant" sets themselves up for success as a leader and for living a life that matters. By leading change that results in positive personal growth, this leader helps to create success for others and success within the organisations they lead.

Extensive, comprehensive and relevant research material is presented in this book with "easy to understand" diagrams helping to simplify the information and make it easily accessible to the reader. There is an excellent "ideas to actions" section at the end of each chapter which acts as a summary and an invaluable resource to help the reader to look inward in order to take outward-facing action and create lasting change.

This is an invaluable book for anyone who wants to create a better version of themselves as a leader and in life. I highly recommend it.

Introduction:
The Leader's Suitcase

Leadership is a journey. Like any journey on which we embark, it is important to be equipped with the things we need to make the trip a positive one. To thrive as a leader, we need to carry with us a Leader's Suitcase that has everything in it that ensures our success, the success of the people we lead, and the success of our organisation. At times, leadership can feel overwhelming, so it is important to not only have our Leader's Suitcase packed, but to have the suitcase organised in such a way that we can quickly locate what we need to lead ourselves, others, and our organisations.

A few years ago, a friend introduced me to packing cells. Sometimes called packing cubes, these individually zipped containers sit inside my suitcase and have revolutionised the way I pack and retrieve things. Packing is now a breeze as I am able to separate the different things I need for a trip into specific packing cells. My gym gear goes in one cell, while my business attire goes in another. No longer do I waste time dredging through all the things in my suitcase to find that elusive pair of socks! Not having to unpack then repack my suitcase as I move from place to place, being able to quickly locate the things I need, has greatly reduced my travelling stress.

In the same way that I use packing cells to organise the things in my physical suitcase, I have used the idea of packing cells to organise my metaphorical Leader's Suitcase. It is so important for leaders to be able to locate the right thing, at the right time, for the right purpose. We never want to be that leader who, in the middle of a crisis, is floundering around trying to locate the thing they need or, worse still, randomly applying different tools in the hope that something will work. Using the notion of packing cells to help us think logically and systematically about what we need to take with us as leaders helps us to better navigate all the twists, turns, and bumps we will encounter on our leadership journey.

To thrive as leaders, it is essential to:

- **Set Yourself Up for Success**
- **Set Others Up for Success**
- **Set Organisations Up for Success.**

And so, in a Leader's Suitcase, we organise our materials and approaches for these different types of success into three packing cells. One cell contains material that sets oneself up for success, one for others, and the final cell has the strategies for organisational success. With these three cells in our Leader's Suitcase, we have everything we need.

The enjoyment and success of a journey is determined by what it is we carry. Without the right things to hand, we end up surviving instead of thriving. Worse still, when leaders are not thriving, then it is likely that the people they work with and their organisation won't be thriving either.

Thriving leaders have in their suitcases everything that ensures the success of themselves, the people they work with, and their organisation. Smart leaders – no matter how experienced – stay smart by always being on the lookout for new items to add to the packing cells in their suitcase, discarding things that are no longer useful. They carefully choose the things most suited to their current leadership context. Knowledge about what effective leaders do continues to grow through the sharing of research findings and the experience of others. We need to continually check that the things in our Leader's Suitcase are up-to-date and relevant.

In the same way that we pack our suitcases ahead of a journey, leaders can pack, in advance, their own Leader's Suitcase. We don't have to wait until we are in a leadership position to start acquiring the resources we will need; we can start packing at any time. In fact, it is often prudent to begin accumulating the material we will need before venturing forth.

Following this are listed the three packing cells that leaders – and those aspiring to become leaders – need to fill in order to be equipped for the journey. Together, as illustrated on the cover of this book, they fill our Leader's Suitcase. This book equips you with the tools and strategies you'll find in *Packing Cell One: Setting Yourself Up for Success*. The second and third books in the series fill packing cells two and three.

Packing Cell One: Setting Yourself Up for Success

The first person every leader leads is themselves. In fact, the mark of an authentic leader is one who uses their own behaviour to exemplify the expectations they hold for others. When we have leadership over our own lives, our life has greater meaning, our values underpin our identity as a leader, and our decisions, boundaries, and habits align with the leader we aspire to be. We utilise our strengths, effectively manage our time and workload, and employ strategies that bring positivity and happiness to our lives.

Whether an experienced leader, someone just starting out on

the leadership journey, or someone aspiring to lead, we have a choice as to whether we thrive or just survive. We may not always be able to control what happens to us, but we can always control our response.

This book draws on many of the theories of positive psychology and weaves them together with sound leadership practices to help us thrive and not just survive as leaders. By the end of this book, you will be clear on the purpose that underpins your leadership and know how to use your personal values to make wise decisions, set and keep boundaries, and develop habits that will enable you to thrive. You will also be armed with an array of strategies to help you tackle every situation in a positive and sustaining manner.

When we set ourselves up for success, we are choosing to positively deviate from the survival mode so many leaders find themselves in today. Thriving as a leader is the best way to ensure the success of those we lead and significantly contributes to the success of our organisations.

Packing Cell Two: Setting Others Up for Success

Packing Cell Two, the second book in this series, equips leaders to lead others. We set others up for success when we lead with empathy and in a way that both supports and challenges everyone to be the best version of themselves.

Authentic relationships, built on trust, sit at the heart of this work. The people we lead need to know they can trust us, and we, in turn, need to be able to trust them. They also need to be able to trust each other. Growing high-functioning teams that work together so that everyone meets their accountabilities is some of the most important work a leader does.

In *Packing Cell Two*, you will discover how to grow the capacity of others using a strengths-based approach. You will understand the importance of relationships that both support and challenge. You will learn how to transform the conversations you once saw as difficult, into opportunities to foster growth, connection, and belonging. You will also learn about how to set team members up to work with each other successfully.

Packing Cell Three: Setting Organisations Up for Success

The goal of the third book is to take many of the strategies and tools from the previous packing cells and to utilise them within the broader organisational context. *Packing Cell Three* will equip you with approaches that will help you affect organisational change, irrespective of your place in the hierarchy.

At the heart of every successful organisation is a compelling vision that gives purpose and meaning to the work. This vision is the glue that binds every part of the organisation together. But having a compelling vision and great culture is not enough. There needs to be a well-thought-out strategy to ensure the vision translates into action. Developing the strategy is the key work of senior leaders, as is identifying and tracking the key priorities needed to deliver the strategy. Operationalising the priorities is the important work of the mid-tier leaders. For a vision to come to life, everyone in an organisation needs to understand their role and be supported in it.

This book will show you how to weave together your organisation's vision, values, mission, and strategy into an approach that sees everyone in your organisation focused on delivering your priorities. It will also equip you with tools and strategies from the field of design thinking to lead change in a way that keeps people at the centre of the process.

While senior leaders hold the ultimate responsibility for

setting their organisation up for success, this packing cell equips *all* leaders to fulfil their roles.

So Let the Journey Begin

This book tackles *Packing Cell One: Setting Yourself Up for Success*.

Packing Cell One contains our individualised resources. When we pack for a real trip, this is the packing cell where we put the things that are rarely seen by others. This is the cell that contains our personal items. It is also the cell that contains the things most critical to the success of any journey.

This book is all about setting ourselves up for success, and is full of fresh ideas and approaches we can deploy to become the leader we aspire to be and that others need us to be. The first person we always lead is ourselves. When we thrive, the people we work with are more likely to thrive, as is the organisation. Thriving as a leader starts with us.

In addition to this book there are Masterclasses you can register for that will help you apply what you learn in this book to your personal leadership journey. The QR code below will take you to further information about this.

THE LEADER'S SUITCASE

Packing Cell One

Setting Yourself Up for Success

1.
Becoming a Positive Deviant

"No matter how far life pushes you down, no matter how much you hurt, you can always bounce back."
- Sheryl Swoopes

Life happens to all of us. Sometimes the things that happen are good; at other times, they are not. Sometimes we can find ourselves in a place where the only thing we have control over is how we respond to what is happening to us. This is the space where we get to choose if the current situation we are navigating will make us arrogant or humble, bitter or better. This is the space where we get to choose to be like everyone else, or to respond differently. Do we become a conformist or a deviant?

Often when we think about the label "deviant", we see it as something bad. It actually isn't. A deviant is simply someone who behaves in a way that is different from the norm, as in something that is usual, typical or standard. A negative deviant is someone whose actions fall below the norm, whereas a positive deviant is someone whose response exceeds it. Negative deviance is a response that falls below the norm, whereas positive deviance is a response that exceeds it. The relationship between norms, and positive and negative deviance, is illustrated in Figure 1.1.

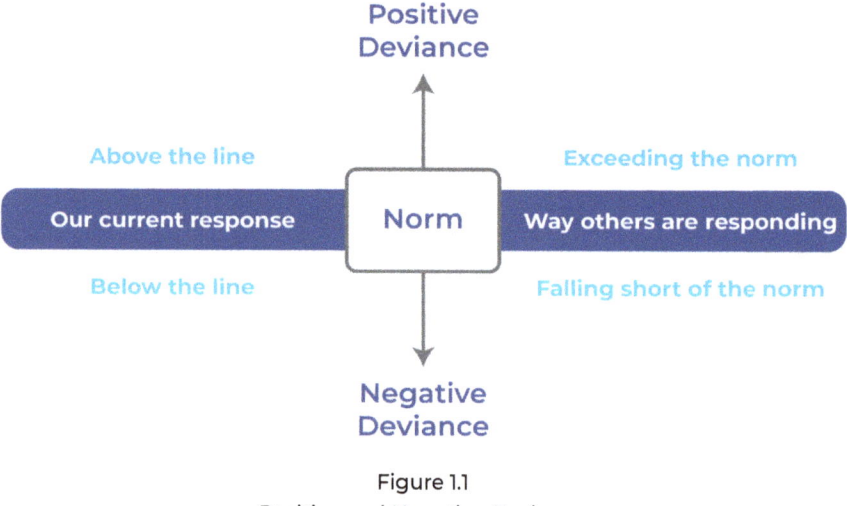

Figure 1.1
Positive and Negative Deviance

Negative and positive deviants really stand out during disasters. Negative deviants are the ones who see a disaster as an opportunity to loot or gain an advantage for themselves. Positive deviants are the ones we celebrate as heroes, those who often risk their lives to save others.

Positive deviance first appeared as a term in nutrition research in the 1970s.[1] Researchers discovered that some parents in an impoverished village used uncommon – but successful – strategies to ensure their children were adequately fed. The strategies included four or five meals a day instead of two, like the rest of the village, and feeding the children food that others thought was only suitable for adults. Like all positive deviants, these parents deviated from what was considered normal practice in their village, achieving a very positive outcome for their children.

Positive deviance is defined by the Positive Deviance Collaborative[2] as:

> *"Positive Deviance (PD) is based on the observation that in every community there are certain individuals or groups whose uncommon behaviors and strategies enable them to find better solutions to problems than their peers, while having access to the same resources and facing similar or worse challenges."*

Humans are wired towards normalising behaviour. In the early days of human civilisation, the best chance of survival was to fit in and find acceptance within a group. Today, we still find that any group that spends enough time together will begin to normalise their behaviour so they reflect each other. Even people who negatively deviate from the accepted standards end up with their own set of social norms. We only need to look to gangs or religious cults to see the truth in this. Attempts to stand out from the crowd simply result in a whole new set of norms being developed and adhered to.

It is, therefore, a very deliberate choice to decide to be a positive deviant. If we want a life that is different to our current one, then we need to make the courageous decision to think and act in new ways. This is not an easy decision to make. Acting differently from our peers can be a challenge. But if we want to be an optimist in a room full of pessimists, then we need to see the glass as half-full, rather than half-empty. If we find ourselves in the company of doomsayers, we need to express a hopeful view of the future. To be an effective leader requires us to act in a way that causes us to positively deviate away from what we are currently experiencing.

As well as positively deviating from our peers, we are also able to positively deviate from ourselves. By this, I mean choosing to act in a way different to what we would usually do. Practices from the past might be worth investigating as potential sources of positive deviation from ourselves. For example, in the past, I have typically taken on the role of a martyr when I have become overwhelmed with work. To positively deviate from this, I need to be willing to accept the help of others. You might be someone who has always managed to fit in doing the housework despite the myriad of other calls on your life; a positive deviation from this expectation would be to employ someone else to do it. If you have always worked across the weekend, then maybe it is time to positively deviate from this practice by nominating one day of the weekend when you don't.

There are many famous positive deviants. Oprah Winfrey is one. Now one of the world's most famous talk show hosts, she grew up in poverty with a single mother who lived on welfare. Oprah was abused as a child, ran away at 13, and got pregnant at 14. She was also fired from her first job for being unfit for television. James Dyson had 5,126 failed prototypes before finally building what would become his famous bagless vacuum cleaner. J.K. Rowling was a broke, depressed single mother, trying to study while writing what are now some of the most famous children's books ever. Walt Disney, Thomas Edison, Albert Einstein; the life and times of so many of our most famous and celebrated people encapsulates what positive deviance is all about. They deviated positively by pressing on when most others would have given up.

In terms of how this relates to leadership, we should remember that we are the first person we lead. Deciding to become a positive deviant is a great way to set ourselves up for success. While much of this work is done on our own, it is also helpful to put ourselves in environments that support our journey. Many leaders have a coach who helps them grow their leadership capabilities. Some leaders belong to a group of like-minded professionals with whom they can share their challenges and find support amongst trusted colleagues. Other leaders add disciplined practices into their lives such as meditation, writing a gratitude diary, or participating in regular exercise to help them positively deviate from their current reality. Whatever we choose, it needs to be something that works for us.

Once we are set up for success, we are better equipped to lead others. A sound principle of leadership is that we should not expect those around us to change unless we are prepared to change ourselves. A couple of great questions to ask are, "How might I need to change in order for this situation I find myself in to change?" and "How might I be contributing to this situation?"

If you are sitting there thinking, "I'm not sure if it is possible to lead and to thrive", then you are not alone. Many of us are merely existing in survival mode because we don't know what else to do.

SURVIVAL MODE

Many leaders are finding themselves lurching from one crisis to the next. The number of crises facing leaders has increased significantly in recent times. This has been driven in part by post-pandemic trauma, the increase of significant weather events caused by global warming, and the uncertainty around the impact of emerging AI digital technologies. The trust that people once indiscriminately placed in professionals is no longer there. Professionals now find themselves in situations where they have to prove themselves trustworthy before they are trusted. Is it any wonder that some leaders feel as though they are just hanging on by their fingernails?

An unfortunate consequence of dealing with one crisis after another is that leaders can experience heightened levels of fear. Fear is an interesting emotion: it is one of our most primal responses, and can be either positive or negative. Positive fear helps keep us safe; it is the emotion that stops us from taking unnecessary risks. It is a negative emotion when it causes us to feel stressed or unable to cope. Fear triggers a physiological response in our bodies, releasing the stress hormones cortisol and adrenaline. It also increases our heart rate and blood pressure. If we are in danger, these physical responses are useful to aid an escape. However, if we are not in danger, a fear response takes blood away from our brain and inhibits our ability to think rationally. This is what puts us into survival mode.

Recognising when we are in survival mode is an important step in our journey to becoming a positive deviant. It is important because when we are in *survival* mode, we are in *react* mode. Responding reactively is a dangerous place for a leader; it is never good to act first and think later. We set ourselves up for success when we create safe spaces from which we can proactively respond.

Sherry Gaba[3], writing for Psychology Today, tells us that when in survival mode, we react in one of four ways - *fight, flight, freeze* or *fawn*. *Fight* and *flight* are well-known responses linked to our hunter-gatherer past when survival depended on the ability to either fight or flee danger. *Freeze* is the state of being rendered incapable of moving or making a choice. *Fawn* is being extremely nice to the person who is the threat in order to gain favour.

The first step to moving from a surviving leader to a thriving one is to recognise when we are operating from a place of survival.

For today's leader, the different survival responses might look like the following:

Fight

In today's world, this is less likely to be a physical response, although, in extreme circumstances, we may notice ourselves clenching different parts of our body as a way of staying in control. Nowadays it is more common to fight with words, both written and spoken. Today's warriors are more likely to wield a keyboard than a sword, with email and social media being the preferred battleground. Leaders in fight mode may write feisty emails. Sometimes leaders in fight mode spend hours composing these angry emails in their heads, even though they know they are unlikely to ever send them.

As well as using writing as a weapon, many people in fight mode attack verbally. Sadly, the target of these attacks can be the ones closest to us, who, if we are not careful, end up getting what is left over at the end of a stressful day. Sometimes, modern fight mode manifests as heated discussions, characterised by people so busy getting their point across, they've forgotten to listen to others. At other times, people choose to fight stealthily, by gossiping, complaining or badmouthing others behind their backs.

Flight

In times past, *flight* probably saw our ancestors fleeing dangerous situations. Nowadays *flight*, like *fight*, is less likely to be a physical reaction. But, if on a dark night you hear a suspicious sound behind you, *run* might well be the choice you make!

The most common way we might exhibit a flight response is when we find ourselves running away from a problem rather than towards it. Sometimes this might be choosing to ignore a situation rather than face up to the facts. It might be convincing ourselves that the issue staring us in the face isn't really an issue at all. It could be withdrawing inside ourselves, or sulking, rather than addressing a relationship issue. It could be actively seeking a new job because the challenges at our current one are just too overwhelming. It might be taking sick days because we just can't face going to work.

Ignoring data or failing to collect data about what is happening in our organisation is another way our flight response might show up. We might find ourselves choosing a place to sit in a meeting where we are unlikely to be called on to contribute, which signals us to realise that we are in flight mode, trying to avoid a situation.

Freeze

In extreme circumstances, we can find ourselves so overwhelmed we can't think straight. When faced with the news of an unexpected death or serious illness, this is understandable. But it can also happen in situations related to our job. The reason we can't think straight is that our brain perceives the threat to be so bad that its thinking part literally stops working in order to redirect all cognitive resources to threat management. A little bit like the ostrich who puts its head in the sand, we choose to wait and see if there is a problem, rather than front-footing situations.

Leaders in *freeze* mode can find themselves unable to think clearly or speak articulately in stressful situations. I once dealt with a person who had a nasty habit of twisting my words to mean something different to what I was communicating. I became so scared of giving them ammunition that I started to stutter!

Being unable to think straight significantly impacts our ability to react. It will be a struggle to clearly articulate thoughts or make decisions.

Fawn

Fawning is going out of our way to please those more powerful than us. It is driven by the belief that if someone likes us, then they will be nice to us. As a survival response, it shows up in many different guises. It might be bending the rules or agreeing to do something you don't want to do in order to appease someone who you know is capable of making trouble. It might be paying more attention to some people than others.

Fawn might be choosing to avoid a conflict, rather than address an issue. Or it might be allowing others to compromise your boundaries in the hope that this will stop them from causing trouble. This might look like responding to emails late at night, or taking phone calls outside of office hours.

Fawn can also be a reluctance to call out someone's bad behaviour. Sometimes the targets of bullies will start acting extra nice to their tormentors in the hope that if they start to like them and can see them as a person, then the bullying behaviour will stop. Sadly, this response does little to stop a bully and often results in an acceleration of the bullying tactics.

Noticing Our Fear

Fear is the emotion underpinning all these survival responses. *Fight, flight, freeze* and *fawn* are the responses we use to mask our fear; but whether it is masked or obvious, it's still there. Our survival instinct causes us to feel fear whenever we sense danger or feel unsafe. Fear might be showing up in our lives as:

- an uncomfortable feeling in our stomach when we go to open our emails
- a surge of anxiety when our caller ID shows us who is calling; or, even worse, every time our phone rings

- lying awake at night, churning over the day's events
- overthinking meetings
- that gurgling feeling in our stomach when we walk into a room
- being unable to think straight or stuttering when we are talking with someone.

Noticing our fear is the first step towards doing something about it. When we notice ourselves responding in any of the ways above, it is time to call a timeout so that we can figure out what is going on, and do something about it. I remember once hearing myself stutter when I bumped into a client at a supermarket. As you may recall me mentioning earlier, this person had an unpleasant habit of twisting my words to mean something I hadn't said. I'd become so anxious about being misquoted that I had started responding from a place of fear. Once I realised this, I was able to do something about it. In this case, I invited the person to meet with me and disclosed my fear about speaking to her. She was absolutely shocked, as she had no idea that she had that impact on people.

Other strategies I have used are:

- adopting Amy Cuddy's[4] 'power pose' ahead of meetings. The theory behind this is that your body position can influence your brain
- thinking about the worst thing that could happen. This may seem counterintuitive, but often thinking about the worst thing that could happen brings much-needed perspective
- talking to a trusted friend or colleague
- doing a mindfulness exercise. Often this is as simple

as focusing on breathing and consciously slowing down exhalation.

Identifying and managing fear is a great short-term solution when we find ourselves surviving rather than thriving, but in the long term, it leaves us stressed and miserable. To set ourselves up for success, we need to replace our survival response with practices that lead to a thriving life. If we want to thrive rather than just survive, then it is time to positively deviate from the life we are currently experiencing. We need to engage with the deliberate practices that this book invites us to place within our Leader's Suitcase. This book – our first packing cell – weaves together the theories and practices from the discipline of positive psychology with the lived experiences of other positive deviants so we may be better equipped to successfully lead ourselves.

THRIVING NOT SURVIVING

"The science and practice of positive psychology offers powerful insights and proven strategies to help individuals, organisations and communities thrive and excel."
- Langley Group[5]

In recent years I have become very interested in positive psychology, a field of psychology that focuses on the things people can do in order to thrive and not just survive. This book draws on many strategies from the discipline of positive psychology, together with my thinking about how leaders might use these to best set themselves up for success. But first, a little bit of background and an introduction to positive psychology.

The study and application of positive psychology began in earnest after the Positive Psychology Summit in 1999. In his speech at the Summit, Martin Seligman[6] sought to change the way people thought about psychology as a healing profession. Where treatment had almost exclusively focused on identifying and targeting weaknesses and issues, his goal was to shift to a greater focus on people's character and strengths. He talked about positive psychology as a way to focus on happiness and subjective experience, as well as positive character, relationships, altruism and positive communities and families.

Over the last 20 years, our knowledge and understanding of positive psychology have continued to grow. In 2011 Seligman published his book *Flourish*,[7] in which he identified and wrote about the five elements of his well-being theory that contributed to human flourishing. These were:

1. Positive Emotion
2. Engagement
3. Relationships
4. Meaning
5. Accomplishment.

The acronym PERMA helps us to remember these elements and different aspects of these are woven throughout the book.

Today the field of positive psychology provides us with a body of evidence about what contributes to life satisfaction, how to be happy despite our personal circumstances, how to experience more positive emotions and what to do about the negative ones, and most importantly, how to live our lives in a way that enables us to thrive and not just survive.

When we think about the struggles the world has gone through in recent times, it is no surprise that well-being is such a significant focus for many. The state of well-being is definitely better than being in a state of ill-being. But positive psychology encourages us to not just aim for well-being, but instead aim for a thriving, flourishing life. It is helpful to see this on a continuum as shown in Figure 1.2.

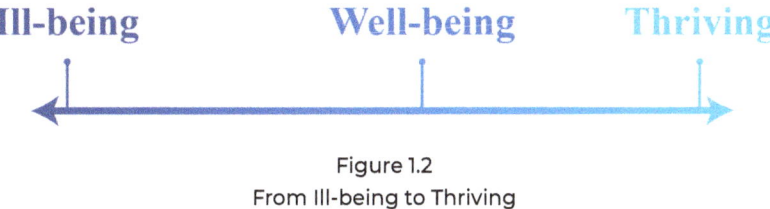

Figure 1.2
From Ill-being to Thriving

We often hear people talk about well-being as if that is an end in itself. But why would we settle for a norm that is just being well when to positively deviate from this would lead to a thriving life? Strategies from the field of positive psychology equip us to live a thriving life. This is positive deviance at its best.

FROM SURVIVING TO THRIVING

To help us make sense of the journey from surviving to thriving, I have developed a model called the Circles of Positive Deviance, and this is shown in Figure 1.3.

The Leader's Suitcase: Setting Yourself Up For Success

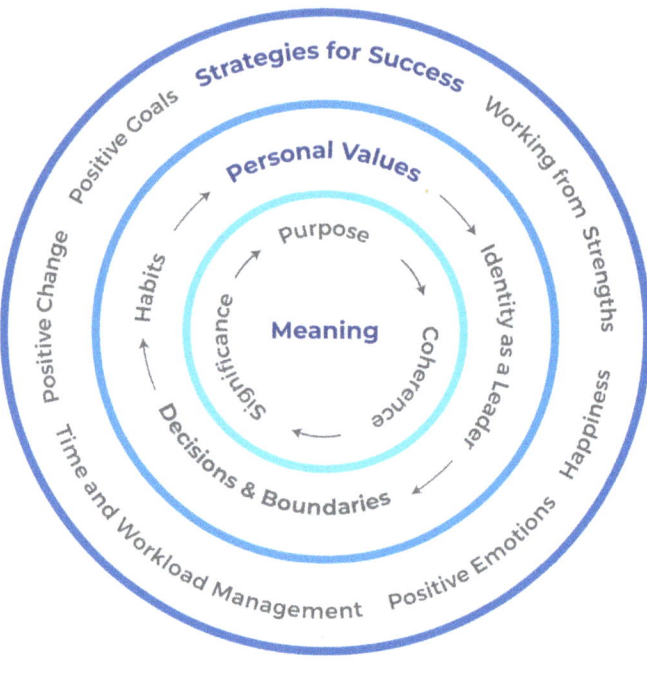

Figure 1.3
Circles of Positive Deviance

The three Circles of Positive Deviance are based on Simon Sinek's[8] Golden Circles of Why, How, What. They act as our guide throughout this book as we positively deviate from the life we are currently living.

At the centre of the Circles of Positive Deviance is the "why" for our leadership. This is Meaning, or more specifically, the meaning we bring to our lives. Meaning is a fundamental component of well-being and flourishing.[9,10]

Researchers from the field of positive psychology identify three things that help people to find meaning in their lives: purpose, coherence, and significance.[11] Purpose is about the core aims and aspirations we have for our life; coherence is about making sense of our life and is the cognitive component of meaning; and significance is about living a life that matters, bringing an evaluative component to meaning in life. These three components come together to give us meaning – the innermost layer in the Circles of Positive Deviance. This gives us our "why" for leadership, and is explored in more depth in Chapter Two.

The second circle details "how" we thrive as leaders. This comes from knowing our personal values and using this knowledge to craft our identity as a leader. When we are clear about our identity as a leader, we are able to make decisions, set and keep boundaries, and form habits that reinforce our personal values and take us closer to the leader we aspire to be.

> *"He (sic) who has a why to live for*
> *can bear almost any how"*
> *- Friedrich Nietzsche*

The third circle is "what" we can do as leaders to positively deviate from our current experiences. These strategies for success combine practices from the field of positive psychology with my leadership experience to help us positively deviate towards a thriving life. They are strategies we pull out of our Leader's Suitcase on a regular basis.

We will dig into each circle in greater detail in future chapters.

CHAPTER SUMMARY
Becoming a Positive Deviant

A deviant is someone who deviates from the usual or typical way of behaving. A positive deviant's response exceeds the norm.

Positive psychology is the field of psychology that helps us understand what contributes to life satisfaction. It outlines how to be happy despite personal circumstances, how to experience more positive emotions and what to do about the negative ones, and how to live life in a way that enables us to thrive and not just survive.

When we are living in survival mode, we are in a reactionary state. Fear is the emotion underpinning all our survival responses. To set ourselves up for success, we need to counter our survival response with practices that the science of positive psychology has shown to lead to a thriving life.

The Circles of Deviance helps us make sense of the journey from surviving to thriving. The inner circle is the "why" of our leadership and is about meaning. The second circle is the "how" and explores the role our personal values play in our identity as a leader, and our decisions, boundaries and habits. The third circle is the "what". These strategies for success are drawn from positive psychology and the author's leadership experience and provide practical advice about how to achieve a thriving life.

The best way to set ourselves up for success as a leader is to choose to thrive. We do this by positively deviating from many of our current practices in every aspect of our life.

FROM IDEAS TO ACTION

- Think about a time when you positively deviated from the norm. It might be that you decided to take a different approach to a situation than what you normally would, or that you decided to 'not go along with the crowd' and ended up with a better result. What caused you to positively deviate? How did you feel at the time compared to how you feel now as you look back on that situation?

- What is your go-to survival mode response? Is it *fight*, *flight*, *freeze* or *fawn*? How do you recognise yourself going into survival mode? Can you identify some situations which are more likely than not to trigger a survival response?

- When did fear last show up in your life? How did your body respond? What did you do to address it?

2.

Meaning

"The two most important days in your life: the day you were born and the day you discover why."
- Ernest T. Campbell

Meaning sits in the very centre of the inner Circle of Positive Deviance and is fundamental to well-being and flourishing.[12,13] Understanding how meaning applies to our past, present and future lives, sets us up to thrive and not just survive, as leaders.

How meaning is brought to life varies from person to person. It is not something that just appears; it is something we continuously create. Meaning, which gives us the 'why' for our leadership, sits in the centre of the Circles of Positive Deviance (Figure 2.1).

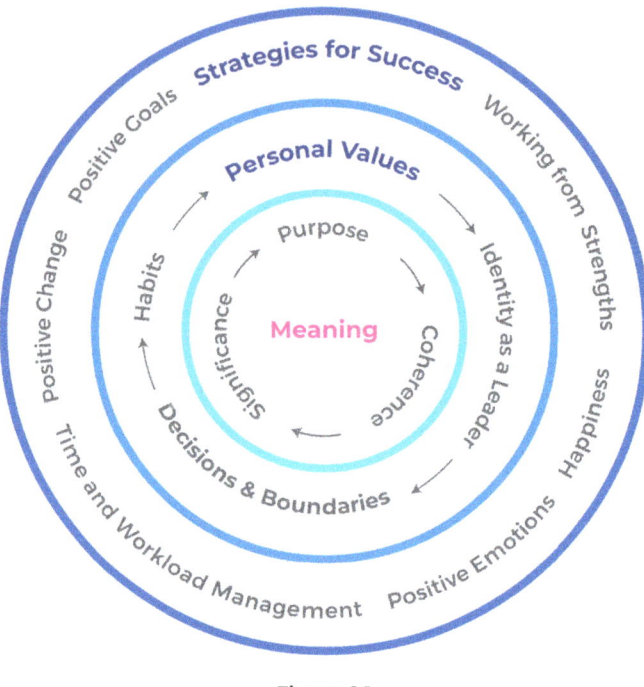

Figure 2.1
Circles of Positive Deviance

Meaning evolves throughout our lives in response to our experiences and beliefs. In times of crisis, meaning is like an oxygen mask on a plane: best fitted on ourselves before assisting others.

> *"For the meaning of life differs from man to man (sic), from day to day and from hour to hour. What matters, therefore, is not the meaning of life in general, but rather the specific meaning of a person's life at a given moment"*
> – Viktor E. Frankl[14]

It is helpful to think about meaning in life as having three interrelated components: purpose, coherence, and significance.

Purpose encompasses our core aims and the aspirations we hold for our lives. It is the motivation for what we do.

Coherence enables us to make sense of our life by connecting our current endeavours with the bigger picture. It is the cognition we bring to living a life of meaning.

Significance focuses on living a life that matters. It is the inherent value we see in our lives. Significance evaluates our impact and helps us to know that we are making a difference and what this difference looks like.

The three components of meaning interrelate, as shown in Figure 2.2.

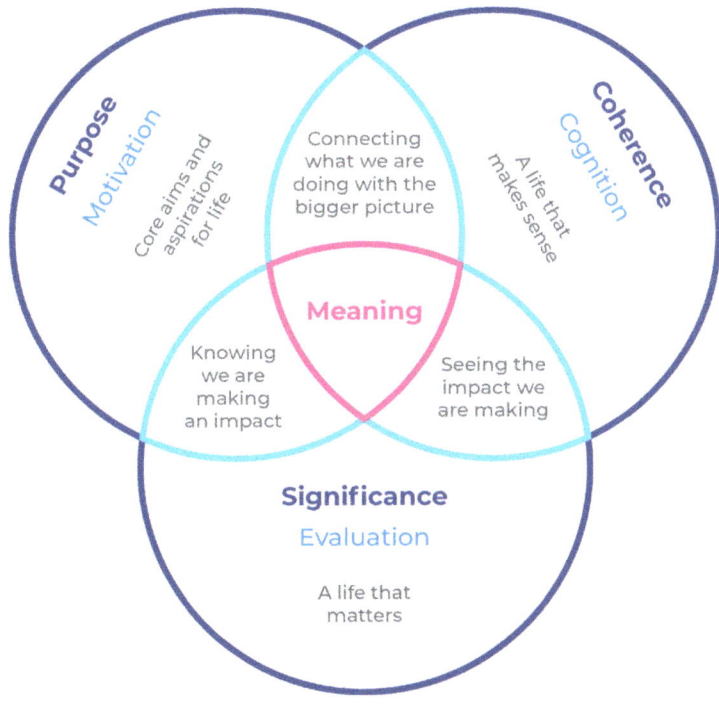

Figure 2.2
The Components of Meaning

We are now going to explore the three components of meaning in greater depth. We are beginning with *purpose*, because unless we are clear about our purpose, it is very difficult to bring coherence to our work and see the significance of what we do. We are then going to look at *the Hero's Journey*, a mythological framework for storytelling, in order to see the coherence and significance of our lives.

PURPOSE

A key to thriving as a leader is knowing our purpose. We need to understand our calling – the thing we were put on this earth to achieve. A way to think about calling, is to identify what it is that brings us deep gladness and what the world needs. If you are not currently able to identify your calling, then don't panic. You're in great company, as it is thought around 50% of leaders struggle to articulate the purpose of their lives.

Jim Collins, in his book *BE 2.0*,[15] uses an ancient Greek parable that compares foxes and hedgehogs to define purpose. Collins contrasts the many strategies foxes use to escape danger with the one strategy a hedgehog always uses. He believes that in the world of leadership, the hedgehog always wins because having only one strategy means that the hedgehog is never tempted to stray from what it understands its core purpose to be. While some may argue that the fox with many strategies has the advantage, especially at times of great uncertainty, the fox is also in danger of pursuing things that are misaligned with its purpose.

According to Collins, we discover our purpose at the intersection of three things: what we are deeply passionate about, what we can be the best at in the whole world, and what best drives our economic engine. As leaders, the sooner we understand what our purpose is, the better. Knowing our purpose and then only accepting roles that help us to fulfil it ensures we experience meaning in our jobs.

Let's take a dive into the three things Collins asks us to consider to help identify or confirm our purpose.

What Are You Deeply Passionate About?

Here, Collins is talking about the thing which gets us out of bed every morning and keeps us awake at night. There will be many things in our lives that we are passionate about, but in this instance, we need to identify what is our most deeply-held passion. For me, it is about equipping others to be successful. As I look back over my life, I have seen this passion expressed in many different ways. As a teenager, I spent my holidays as a leader on summer camps for disadvantaged children. Then I became a teacher, a principal, a subject-matter expert in an IT company, a facilitator in the use of design thinking to effect organisational change, coaching and mentoring leaders, and running Masterclasses. Whilst these are all quite varied jobs, at the heart sits the same deeply-held passion for equipping others to be successful.

So, what is the deeply-held passion that sits at the heart of your leadership? If you are unsure, here are a couple of things to think about which might help.

1. Observe yourself when you are talking with others about your work.

Notice what it is you are talking about when you feel lit up or energised. Think about the things that others seek your input about and the things you enjoy talking through. Also, ask yourself if there is anything you feel put out about if not included.

2. Identify the times in your life when you enter a state of flow.

We've all experienced times of flow in our life. This is a state when we are so lost in our work that time and place no longer matter. Hungarian-American psychologist, Mihaly Csikszentmihalyi,[16] describes flow as "a state in which people are so involved in an activity that nothing else seems to matter; the experience is so enjoyable that people will continue to do it even at great cost, for the sheer sake of doing it."

What were you doing the last time you were in flow? What is it you are doing when you suddenly look at your watch and realise that a whole lot of time has passed? I go into flow whenever I am writing, so much so that before I start, I set an alarm on my phone to remind me when it is time to stop. Marc Anthony, an American musician, once said, "If you do what you love, you'll never work a day in your life."

Being able to articulate our most deeply held passion is a critical component in identifying the purpose of our life.

What Can You Be The Best In The World At?

This isn't talking about *being* better than everyone else. It is talking about the thing we *do* better than most. What is it that we are able to do better than anyone else in the room?

> *An example of contrasting talents occurred during my positive psychology training, when we came back from lunch to find our workshop room filled with tables covered in paints, paper and a whole array of creative materials. At each person's place was a blank canvas block. Our task was to take the supplied materials and use them to represent our strengths. There are many things I am good at, but using visual art to represent my strengths is not one of them! I initially felt quite intimidated by this task. However, I'm good at writing and I'm energised by focusing on detail. So, I grabbed a brush and some paint, and covered my blank canvas by describing all my*

strengths using words. This was a choice I made to lean into the task, using a talent at which I am better than most.

To help pinpoint what we are most talented at, it can be useful to think about the role we often take in a group. Are we the person that the rest of the group naturally looks to, to take the lead? Are we the one who always makes sure there are enough seats? Are we the person who offers to organise things on behalf of others?

Look back over the years and identify the one big thing that you have always done, probably in a variety of ways and in lots of different situations. This might very well be a signpost to your purpose.

The thing that I am the best in the world at, is taking seemingly disconnected ideas and applying them in ways that make sense. This is why I have always been able to figure out how emerging technologies might be used in different contexts. It is also why I've ended up writing a book that is pulling lots of different leadership strategies into one Leader's Suitcase.

What Drives Your Economic Engine?

Lots of people have many great ideas. However, unless we can figure out how to make money from them or how we are going to resource them, they will only ever stay as good ideas. Sadly, it is not enough to be passionate about and good at something in order to experience success. We need to make it work financially as well.

When Collins first asked the question about what drives our economic engine, it was within the context of business, where a product or service is offered, and someone else buys it. As people engaged with his ideas, Collins realised that the same was not true in organisations such as schools or hospitals. There, it was not about figuring out how to get others to buy a product or service, but about having sufficient resources in order to bring the idea to life.

In the course of my work, I have had lots of conversations with extraordinary people who have amazing ideas. It always fascinates me to observe the reaction when I bring the conversation around to money. People who are passionate about something, often forget that their passion is not shared by everyone. We often see this with school leaders who want businesses to sponsor conferences, and are then quite surprised to discover that these companies actually expect schools to buy from them. When the work we do comes from a deeply-held passion or calling, it can be easy to forget that not everyone sees our work that way. This leads to the second problem: people can become blinded by their passion, leading them to believe "if they build it, they will come." The reality is that most "overnight successes" have come from years of hard work and focused dedication.

Your Leadership Purpose

To be set up for ultimate success, our purpose will meet all three of Collin's criteria. There is little point in spending time chasing a passion we are unable to fund. Spending our life pursuing something we are not interested in nor good at will lead to a dissatisfied life. A thriving life comes from doing something we are passionate about, and something we are good at that can be funded.

Organisations also need a purpose. We will delve into this a bit more deeply when we explore the third packing cell of Setting Organisations Up for Success. The closer our personal purpose is aligned to our organisational purpose, the more we will thrive as a leader.

COHERENCE

Coherence is about making sense of the life we are living. Over the course of our lives, our purpose can take many shapes and be expressed in different ways. For example, if someone's purpose was to help people set up and run successful businesses, then they might start out as an accountant, then become a business coach and then a company director. These are three completely different roles, but all fulfil the same purpose. Coherence is about connecting what we are currently doing with the bigger picture we hold for our lives.

I started my career as a teacher. This is not surprising, as I have always seen my purpose as equipping others with the tools they need to be successful. Through a combination of study and opportunities, I eventually became a principal, a role I held for 12 years, at two very different schools.

In 2013 my career took an unexpected turn when I was approached to be a member of the senior leadership team of a company our government had created, to enable all New Zealand schools to be connected to high-speed internet. I took the role. At first glance, it may appear odd that I would go from principal of a school to a senior leader in a start-up IT company. But, remembering my purpose, which is to equip others with the tools to be successful, you can see the coherence between my different positions.

You are now reading the first of three books I've authored, which are all about equipping leaders to be successful. Choosing roles connected to my purpose continues to be a priority for me.

It is important to live a life of coherence, because this allows us to meaningfully align our current endeavours within our life's purpose. It also enables us to see the impact we are having which leads to a life of significance; a life that matters. Coherence ensures that we make choices that are consistent with our overarching aims and aspirations for our lives, and it sets us up to align our actions with our personal values; the latter being critical to the identity of the leader we aspire to be. We explore this more in the next chapter on values.

SIGNIFICANCE

In order to thrive and to experience a life of positive deviance, we need to know that our life has significance and that it matters. Significance is the subjective evaluation we make about our experiences and actions. This interpretation can be derived from a variety of sources, including relationships, work, recreational pursuits, and our spirituality. Feeling significant leads to a sense of belonging and connection to others.

> *"Significance may give people a sustained motivation to retain and to keep working towards their purpose."*
> *- Martela & Steger*

Significance helps us locate meaning in life by helping to identify the specific impact we are making and gives us assurance that as we work to fulfil life's purpose, we are making a difference.

 Every Thursday morning, I have a blog post that goes out to hundreds of subscribers. Aptly named Thursday Thinking, my

blog is a collection of thoughts and reflections having to do with leadership.

After every blog post, my inbox is filled with emails from people who have read Thursday Thinking and taken the time to let me know that something has resonated with them, or that they had reflected on an aspect of their leadership as a result of what I have written.

The feedback I get about my blog assures me that the time I spend each week writing and publishing my blog is making a difference. My blog is also another way I am able to fulfil my purpose.

At the beginning of this chapter, we looked at meaning as the intersection between purpose, coherence and significance. Meaning is also closely tied to the stories we tell about ourselves. A group of researchers[17] used *the Hero's Journey*, a form of cultural narrative, as a tool for people to re-story their experiences in a coherent and significant way. They found that the way people choose to tell their stories impacts the meaning they bring to their lives.

THE HERO'S JOURNEY

Joseph Campbell first wrote about *the Hero's Journey* in 1949. He discovered that most stories and myths follow the same narrative pattern. *The Hero's Journey* always starts with a protagonist who embarks on a quest or journey. They face challenges and obstacles which they overcome, to ultimately emerge transformed by their experiences.

"This points to the powerful influence that our life stories have, shaping both our perceptions of our past and our approach to the future."[18]

I have adapted the concept of Campbell's *Hero's Journey* as shown in Figure 2.3 to help us re-story our narrative about leadership.

Figure 2.3
Adapted Hero's Journey for Leadership Narrative

To help make sense of the figure above, here is my story about principalship - a hero's journey that started in the 1990s and finished 10 years ago.

> *As the hero (1) of my own story, my journey to principalship started in the mid-1990s when I was a primary school teacher. Several people told me I was 'principal material' (whatever*

that means!) (2) and I kept telling them that all I wanted to do was be a classroom teacher (Refusal). In 1999, I became a teaching deputy principal of a small rural school in Canterbury. Throughout that year the principal kept telling me that I could be the next principal of the school (2). I used to laugh at his suggestion (Refusal). At the end of that year, the principal resigned. The Board asked me to consider acting in the role of principal (2). I wasn't keen but my husband suggested I give it a go. His words were: "It might be the only chance you get, and you never know, you might be good at it" (3). I reluctantly agreed but I remember almost crying on the first day of school when I had an office, not a classroom! I was still in the refusal stage though, as the role I had taken on was only an acting one; and I was counting the days until I was back with my class.

Several weeks into my acting principal role, the rural leadership advisor visited my school (these people used to exist, but no longer!). He asked me if I was going to apply for the role. I said no (Refusal). He suggested that if I didn't apply for the role, then the chances were I could end up working with someone less skilled than me. He added that if I applied for the role and was unsuccessful then at least I'd be working for someone more skilled than myself (3). I applied and was successful in getting the role (4). This was when I moved from my Known World (teaching) to my Unknown World (school leadership).

It didn't take long for the challenges to start (5). For one thing, being a principal felt so different to being a teacher and I wasn't quite sure how I was supposed to act or how I could influence what was going on in classrooms. But, I was incredibly fortunate to be surrounded by other principal colleagues who made themselves available to me whenever I needed them (6). I was also blessed with a highly supportive Board (6). I started to experience some victories (7). Then, I was appointed as project director for a local cluster of schools and asked to share our school's story at an Australasian conference (7).

Time moved on, and I left that school to become the principal of a large urban school in Wellington (4-7). At first, I circled back to stage 4, but the Known World was more encompassing than when I first became principal. Once again, I was surrounded by allies, in the form of principal colleagues and supportive Board members; and once again, we saw many victories. Over time, I discovered that I intuitively knew how to respond to most situations I encountered (8). The last step in my Hero's Journey came in the final 18 months of my last principalship. I realised that I had stopped acting like a principal, and the way I lead had started to be closely aligned with the person I was when I was a teacher (9).

Taking the time to re-story our leadership journey is a useful strategy with which to uncover greater meaning in our lives. As we think about other leadership stories we could tell using the adapted *Hero's Journey*, we get a new perspective on what we've done and achieved and faced in our journeys. Of course, not every story, including my own, follows *the Hero's Journey* by the strict outline shown in Figure 2.3. Some journeys emphasise different stages more than others.

Meaning, often found through the stories we tell, gives us the "why" for our leader's journey and is the key that unlocks the door to thriving and not simply surviving.

"Meaning is at its heart an integrating factor for people. Meaning pulls together people's ideas about who they are, the kind of world they live in, and how they relate to the people and environments around them."
- Michael Steger[19]

CHAPTER SUMMARY
Meaning

Meaning is a fundamental component of well-being and flourishing, and is something we continuously create.

There are three interrelated components to meaning: purpose, coherence, and significance.

Leaders find purpose at the intersection of what they are passionate about, what they are the best in the world at, and what they can resource.

Coherence is about making sense of the life we are living. It is about connecting what we are currently doing with the bigger picture we hold for our lives.

Significance is the subjective evaluation we make about experiences and actions in order to live a life that matters.

Meaning is closely tied to the stories we tell about ourselves. *The Hero's Journey* is a cultural narrative that is a useful tool with which to frame experiences in a positive and cohesive way. Using the adapted *Hero's Journey* (Figure 2.3) to re-story our leadership experiences impacts the meaning we bring to our lives.

FROM IDEAS TO ACTION

- How confident are you in articulating what the purpose is for your life? Have a go at figuring out your purpose using the Hedgehog Concept, by drawing three intersecting circles. In one circle, write what it is you are passionate about; in the second circle, write what you are better than most at; and in the third circle, write what you are either resourced to do or can make money out of. Now look at all three circles and come up with your purpose.

- Have a go at writing your leadership story, using the same narrative pattern as *the Hero's Journey*. Does your story follow *the Hero's Journey*, or does it deviate? Or, maybe it is only partly told?

- How does thinking about your leadership story as a hero's journey help bring coherence and significance to the work you do?

3.
Personal Values

*"Inā kite koe i tētahi mea hē, hakatikangia.
Inā kore ka rite koe ki taua hē.
If you see something wrong in front of you, then correct it
because if you don't, you will become like it."*
- Dame Naida Glavish

Meaning sits at the very heart of the Circles of Positive Deviance.

We experience meaning in our life when we know our purpose, and understand how it brings coherence and significance to our life and our work. Meaning gives us the "why" for our lives. Our next step is to explore the "how". This is the focus of the middle Circle of Positive Deviance (Figure 3.1).

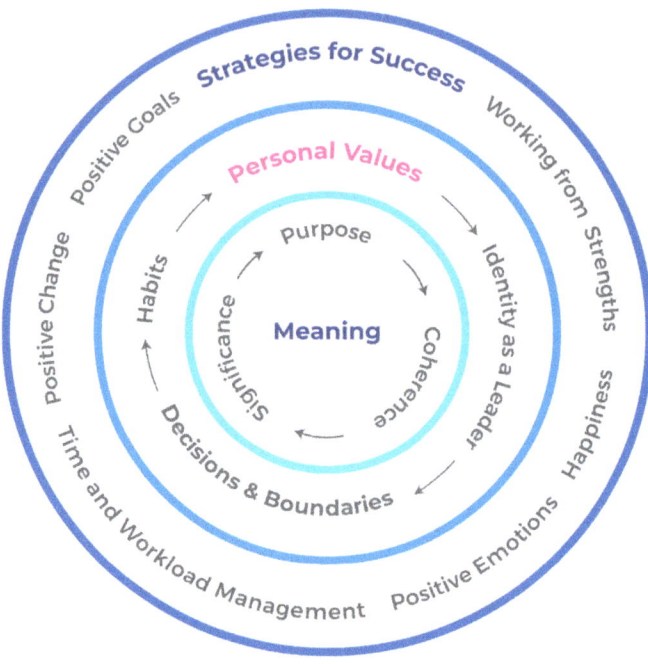

Figure 3.1
Circles of Positive Deviance

How we can use our personal values to craft the identity of the leader we aspire to be is our next focus. It is important for leaders to act in alignment with their values, because this brings authenticity to their life and their work.

Staying with the middle Circle of Positive Deviance, Chapter Three links our values-driven leadership aspirations with the decisions we make and the boundaries we keep. Over time our decisions and boundaries become the habits that reinforce our personal values (Figure 3.2).

And so, the circle is complete. The closer our habits are aligned to our personal values, the easier it is to lead with authenticity and ultimately become the leader we aspire to be.

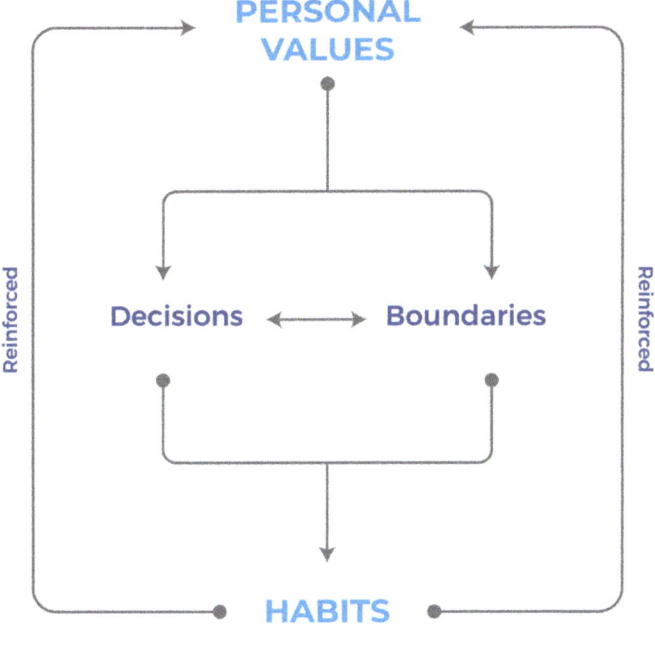

Figure 3.2
The Inter-relationship Between Values and Habits

PERSONAL VALUES

We all have values that guide how we live our lives. They are a representation of who we are and help us to craft the identity of the leader we aspire to be. They are an expression of what matters to us, and are always with us, whether we are aware of them or not. How conscious we are of our values varies from person to person and experience to experience. Many people only become acutely aware when they experience something that doesn't feel quite right, perhaps finding themselves in a situation that is either in conflict with or causes them to question their values. When we take actions to identify our values, we are moving them from our subconscious into conscious thought. Transitioning from having an innate sense of our values, to deeply understanding them, enables us to be fully aligned in the way we live and lead. This is key to the "how" of our leadership and brings meaning to our work.

Most of the time our values act a bit like the cruise control in a car: effortlessly managing what we do in the background. However, cruise control is only safe when we pay attention to setting and re-setting it according to the conditions we encounter. In the same way, our values help us the most when we consciously set and reset how we use them in response to the different situations we encounter. Some things we do, even though they might align with our values, may not be helping us. For example, someone who values adventure might let this get in the way of making a wise decision about their personal safety. On the other hand, we can use our values to guide us in becoming more like the person we aspire to be. For example, if we value honesty, then we tell the truth even if it disadvantages us. Our personal values are most useful when we are consciously aware of them.

Many of our values are a reflection of our upbringing. If we were brought up in a family that loved the outdoors, then we will probably value being in nature. If our family played lots of games together, then we more than likely will value fun. However, some of the values of our upbringing may not be helpful. For example, in my family, we were always told to put others first and ourselves last. Whilst this is generally a good principle to live by, it is also a value that at times, has caused me to say yes to things when for my own well-being, I should have said no.

Our values reflect our age and stage, changing to reflect the passing years and different priorities. As a teenager, I valued being with others so much that finding myself at home with my family on a Saturday night felt like a failure. Now, Saturday night spent at home with family is one of the things I value the most. When we were parenting young children, we definitely valued an hour without them. Now they are grown up and have left home, we value every hour we spend with them.

Finally, values are shaped by our experiences in life. This can be both positive and negative. Trust is an important value to me. Over the years, as a result of some unpleasant experiences, I have learnt that I need to be careful about who I decide to trust. My life experience has also taught me that not everything is black and white, and in fact, there is much richness to be found in the shades of grey in our lives. I now value diversity more than I value being right. This means I am more open to exploring the opinions and beliefs of others. I am also able to see that in many situations there is not just one right way.

Values shape who we are and impact how others perceive us. They inform the guiding principles through which we lead. Values play two key roles in setting us up for success as a leader:

1. They make explicit the things that matter.
2. They enable us to craft the identity of the leader we aspire to be.

MAKING EXPLICIT THE THINGS THAT MATTER

Knowing what our values are and being able to articulate them is an important aspect of setting ourselves up for success. However, many people, when asked, are unable to articulate what their most important values are. An important step on our positive deviant's journey is to move awareness of values from unconscious to conscious thought.

> *"Until you make the unconscious conscious,
> it will direct your life, and you will call it fate."*
> – Carl Jung

Becoming more aware of our values sets us up to make great decisions that consistently align with the things that are important to us. Being unconscious of our values doesn't stop us from making great decisions, but in tricky situations, being able to articulate the value (even if it is just to ourselves) gives us the confidence to know that the decision we are making is the right one. The place we don't want to end up in, is only figuring out what our values are in situations that are inviting us to compromise them.

Take, for example, the following story:

 A newly appointed principal, at their first meeting with the long-standing School Board Chair, is informed that the large urban school doesn't hold elections for its Board members. The principal asks how this can be, as Board elections are enshrined in the Education Act. The Chair informs them that the system they have been using for years is that if more people are nominated than there are places on the Board, then they approach the extra candidates to withdraw their nomination. They then co-opt them onto the Board once the election date has passed. The principal now has to decide if they will go along with the Board's election-avoiding strategy or risk their yet-to-be-established relationship with the Board by refusing to participate in this long-standing practice.

Because the principal is consciously aware that one of their strongly-held values is truth, they know the right thing for them to do is to refuse to condone the actions of the Board

Chair, even though they know this decision will put developing relationships at risk. This story ends with the school holding its first Board election for years and the Board Chair deciding not to stand for another term. How much more difficult would this decision have been for the principal if they were unaware of how strongly they held onto the value of truth?

It is important to note that not every principal in this situation would have made the same decision. It is also important to note that the decision the principal made in the story was the right one for them because it aligned with their values. Another principal may have valued relationships over truth and made the decision to go along with the strategy this time, but make a stand before the next Board election once they'd established a relationship that could weather the challenge. Neither approach is wrong; they are just different.

The most successful leaders are those whose personal values align with their organisation's values. There is often a difference between what an organisation espouses as its values and the values that the people working for the organisation experience. I explore this more when we do a deep dive in *Packing Cell Three: Setting Organisations Up for Success*. One of our deciding factors for taking on a new job should be that the role feels like a good fit for us. When we are consciously aware of our values, we can use this knowledge to explore whether the organisation we are looking to work for operates in a way that aligns with our values. We could ask informal questions of other employees that we meet and notice how people treat each other. We need to work hard to avoid taking on a role that ends up with us having to work in a way that compromises our values.

From time to time, especially when a new senior leader appointment triggers a re-structure, an organisation's values can change. During this season of change, it is wise to stay alert as to whether or not the proposed new way of operating aligns with your personal values. If it doesn't and the new structure means you have to take on a re-shaped role, think very carefully before accepting it, as redundancy might be the better choice. People burn out very quickly in situations that cause them to operate in a way that is misaligned with their values.

> *"A job is about a lot more than a paycheck.*
> *It's about your dignity. It's about respect.*
> *It's about your place in your community."*
> *- Joe Biden*

If you are unable to name your most strongly held values, or you think they may have changed since you last thought about them, then here are three ways to move your understanding from unconscious to conscious.

1. Respond & Reflect

Here are some questions that, based on your answers, will help you to pinpoint your most strongly held values. I've given you my response to the first question to model the process.

1. If you could choose anything at all to do today, what would it be? Why did you choose this?

   I'd choose to grab a book, a beach towel, my sunscreen, and some yummy snacks, then head with my partner to our favour-

ite beach. The reason I have chosen this is that it describes a great chance to spend time together.
Values reflected: Love and Pleasure.

I'm also thinking about how these values reflect my age and stage. Many years ago, I wouldn't have grabbed a book and beach towel, it would have been my scuba diving gear. My values were once more about adventure than pleasure. In the future, if we're lucky enough to have grandchildren, then it might be buckets and spades I grab (along with the grandchildren) rather than a book, which signifies my values changing more towards my family.
Values reflected: Adventure and Family

Now it is your turn. Here are some questions to get you started:

1. If you could choose anything at all to do today, what would it be? Why did you choose this?
2. What activities do you voluntarily spend time on?
3. What skills do you have that you enjoy sharing with others?
4. Think back to the last time you were in a state of flow. What were you doing?
5. Who has had an impact on your life and why?
6. When do you feel most satisfied?
7. What would you struggle to live without?
8. What is guaranteed to make you grumpy?

Sometimes I get stuck on naming values. When this happens, I do a quick internet search which then provides many useful lists.

2. Online Assessments

If a pen-and-paper reflection isn't your style, then there are lots of values assessments you can take using online tools. I'd recommend a values profile from Psychology Today,[20] or the one found at Personal Values (personalvalu.es).[21] Most of these sites offer a free version of your results, or you can pay to get a more in-depth analysis. With any of these tools, it pays to weigh the results against what you know to be true. You should feel validated by the results, and not surprised.

3. Decision Reflection

At the end of each day, take five minutes to write down the key decisions you have made that day. Assess them as to whether you found them easy or hard to make. Record the values that underpinned the decisions you made. Do this over several days to see what pattern emerges.

Being conscious of our values means that we are able to be deliberate in how we go about doing our job, enabling us to act in a way that strongly resonates with the person we aspire to be.

IDENTITY AS A LEADER

Once we have a clear, conscious understanding of our values, we are in a position to craft our identity as a leader. This is important work because great leaders are made, not born. Great leaders work on themselves, being very mindful of how others are impacted by the way they lead. Being deliberate about crafting our identity means we get to decide how the people in our team will experience our leadership.

Personal Values

The following process is one I use with leaders to help them craft their aspirational leadership identity. If you've never clarified how you use (or aspire to use) your values to fulfil your purpose, then here is a process you could try.

1. Write down your top six values. Beside each value, jot down how they play out when you are at your best and at your worst. For example, here is how one of my values plays out at my best and worst:

Value	Best Case	Worst Case
Wisdom	Sharing my knowledge gained through theory and experience in a way that allows others to choose whether to follow my advice or not.	Coming across as a "know-it-all" - the only one with the right answer.

Figure 3.3
Best and Worst Values

2. Using your best and worst examples, write some declarations that reflect the identity you seek to have as a leader. Here is my example to show you what it might look like. Remember, my purpose is to equip others to be successful.

Value	Best Case
Wisdom	I use my life experiences to help others. I make space for others to show their wisdom.
Honesty	I am kind even when being honest. I speak the truth no matter what the circumstances.
Meaningful work	I prioritise making others successful, over making a profit. I give people tools that enable them to grow their capability.
Love	I work in the interests of others. I am motivated by love when taking action.
Justice	I speak with wisdom and with fairness. I make decisions that are fair to all.
Collaboration	I do things with people, not to people. I build bridges, not walls.

Figure 3.4
Personal Values and Declarations

3. Validate your declarations by testing them against the meaning in your life. Will your declarations take you closer to your purpose? Do they help you make sense of the life you live? Will they make your life matter more or less?

4. Keep your declarations somewhere handy, so you can remind yourself of them on a regular basis.

I'd love to be able to say that I meet all my declarations every day, but like everyone else, I am still a work in progress. These declarations, however, are powerful. They inspire me to be better every day. They give me something to aim for and a way to measure my progress. They remind me of why I do what I do, anchoring me to my purpose. Last but not least, they inspire me to be who I want to be, which is especially helpful during challenging times. I cannot count how many times I have been able to change my response to a situation simply by repeating one of my declarations over and over again, until I believed it!

Declarations re-focus our thinking, from what we do as a leader, to who we are as a leader. For example, working collaboratively is important to me, and so as you can see from the list above, one of my declarations is that I build bridges, not walls. In my early years of leading a school, I was grateful that I had crafted this declaration before I actually needed to apply it. Here's what happened.

My first principalship was in a small rural school, situated in a highly conservative area. Until I arrived, the school had only ever had male principals. All of the other schools in the district were led by males. My fellow principals were all lovely people, but what they didn't realise is that they often acted in a way that made it feel like our local principals' group was more of a boys' club than a professional association. They often made decisions that impacted my school outside of our formal meetings. It was frustrating, because I think they honestly believed that this way of making decisions was doing everyone a favour.

On one particular day, I remember being called to a meeting about a decision that affected our school, but had been made at an informal boys' club meeting (code for the local public bar where only men drank). My frustration at once again being "done to" by my colleagues had turned to anger, but I also knew that if I arrived at the meeting in this state of mind, I'd risk doing more harm than good to an already tenuous relationship. I still remember angrily gripping the steering wheel as I drove, saying over and over to myself, "I build bridges, not walls. I build bridges, not walls." By the time I got to the meeting, I'd made this declaration so many times, I'd brainwashed myself into believing it! This put me in the right frame of mind to objectively tackle the issue and not distance myself further from my colleagues.

The reason why declarations work, such as my "I build bridges, not walls", is that the action of repeating them over and over again develops a neural pathway in our brains. Over time this neural pathway triggers an automated response that is aligned with our values. Not having to think about how we will respond reduces our cognitive load, giving us the space to think more clearly about situations we are facing.

Declarations, once crafted, need to be displayed in a way that ensures they are noticed often. Having a constant reminder of the leader we aspire to be helps moderate our behaviour in situations where our values might start to play against us. They keep us on the path to becoming a positive deviant. For example, one of my values is honesty. This means that whenever I am asked for an opinion about something, my natural instinct is to tell it exactly as I see it. This does not always go well. If, instead, I temper my value of honesty with my value of wisdom, then my declaration becomes, to tell the truth with wisdom. This response preserves the identity I seek as a leader, and at the same time, gives deeper meaning to my life.

CHAPTER SUMMARY
Values

Values are a representation of who we are. We use our personal values to identify the things that matter and to craft the identity of the leader we aspire to be.

Values are shaped by our upbringing, age and stage, and life experiences. They can change over time.

Values play two key roles in setting ourselves up for success.

1. They make explicit the things that matter.
2. They enable us to craft the identity of the leader we aspire to be.

We use our personal values to write declarations that help us re-focus our thinking from what we do as a leader to who we are as a leader.

Declarations create neural pathways in our brains that, over time, trigger an automated response that is aligned with our values. This response preserves the identity we seek as leaders and gives deeper meaning to our lives.

FROM IDEAS TO ACTION

- Identify your six top personal values and write them down. Beside each one jot down how they play out when you are at your best and at your worst.

- Have a go at writing some declarations that reflect the leader you aspire to be. Keep these declarations somewhere handy as a way to remind yourself to try them out. How do your declarations inspire you to be a better leader every day?

4.

Decisions, Boundaries, and Habits

"The decisions you make are a choice of values that reflect your life in every way."
- Alice Waters

The previous chapter explored how being consciously aware of our values helps to make explicit what matters. It also looked at how we can use our values to create declarations that reflect the identity of the leader we aspire to be. This chapter focuses on how to use our declarations to make decisions and set boundaries that reflect the leadership identity we are creating. Over time, consistent decision-making and boundary-holding grow into the habits that enable us to positively deviate from our current life, into one in which we thrive.

DECISIONS

Leaders make decisions in response to hundreds of situations every day. Using our declarations to remind ourselves about our leadership identity means our responses are authentic because they are aligned with our values.

I'll never forget how devastated I felt the day I walked into my boss's office to tell him I was pregnant with my first child. I expected that he would congratulate me on my news; instead, his response was, "You're not!" I replied, "I am", and walked out. I didn't appreciate the message that I had somehow let him down by getting pregnant. Later that day, he did offer his congratulations, but I will always remember the feeling his initial response conveyed. He clearly valued me as a teacher over me as a person. As leaders, we don't always have the luxury of time to decide how we are going to respond in a situation. The clearer we are about our personal values and the declarations that come from these, the easier it is to respond in a way that reflects the leader we aspire to be.

Keeping our values and declarations at the centre of our decision-making is important for consistency. Leaders who are consistent in their decisions experience high levels of relational trust. I think of another boss who, upon learning that my father was ill in the hospital, told me to go. She knew my mother needed me, and they would figure out how to cover my absence. I remember thinking, as I walked out of her office, how unsurprised I was at her response. She was a leader who lived aligned with her values and benefitted from the high relational trust she had with staff.

Not every decision we make is going to be a popular one. However, if our decisions are aligned with our values, then even if others don't like them, we will feel confident that the decision we have made is the correct one. An important step in every leader's journey is being comfortable with knowing that not all people will like what they do all the time. Make no mistake: the first few times a leader's popularity takes a hit, it is tough, especially if they have risen through the ranks and it is their colleagues who are disappointed in them. In time though, leaders accept that the right decision, the one that aligns with who they are as a leader, is far more important than the decision that retains their popularity.

Many decisions are easy, but every now and then, we come across one that we need to take time over. One of the first things to do when faced with a hard decision is to ascertain exactly when the decision needs to be made. Many decisions are not as urgent as others portray them to be. It is my experience that having time to explore different possibilities always results in better decisions. It also gives time to explore any downstream effects of the decision being made.

Decision-making, however, is not a game to play on our own. While the decisions we make should reflect our identity as a leader, we are not the only ones who should be deciding about or benefitting from the decisions being made. As much as possible, we need to involve the people who will be impacted by the decision, in the decision. Giving plenty of opportunity for others to have input about decisions is important, as is being very clear about how a decision is to be made and who will make it. This reduces the opportunity for people to accuse us of not listening simply because we didn't do what they suggested.

Another tip for great decision-making is to use past experiences while remaining open to new ways of doing things. Just because something worked in the past doesn't mean it is the right thing to do in every situation. My experience with Google Maps is a good way to think about this.

> *I travel a lot for my job, and when I'm in an unfamiliar place, I rely heavily on Google Maps to get me to where I need to be, in the shortest possible time. However, I'm not always so obedient if I am driving in familiar territory and have a plane to catch!*
>
> *One night, I ended up leaving for the airport 15 minutes later than I had planned. I wasn't too worried, as I had built in time for having something to eat prior to catching my flight. I didn't need Google Maps to tell me how to get there, as I knew the route. However, I did punch in my destination just to get an update on my predicted arrival time. Google came up with the message, "This is now the fastest route to avoid road closures", and it was not directing me where I'd expected.*
>
> *Being familiar with the normal route, I thought I'd test this theory by not following Google's new direction initially. But, after a bit of driving, Google was still directing me to take the next right off the main road. I reluctantly turned right. The signposts read a different town to the one where the airport was, but I had to trust that I was indeed on the fastest route. I did make my flight, and I also later found out the main road was closed due to a vehicle accident. The lesson in this for me was that if I'd just relied on my past experience and not been open to a different solution, I would have missed my flight.*

It is important to listen to wise counsel from those whom we trust, but it is also important to listen to what our gut is telling us. Intuition, that feeling in our gut about what is right, is an unconscious response that draws on past experiences, and it is worth attending to! We need to be disciplined about not overthinking situations; otherwise, we risk talking ourselves out of the best way to do something. When I catch myself starting to overthink things, I find it useful to trust my instincts and to focus on my successes, rather than dwell on my failures. Take parallel parking, for example:

I'd always prided myself on my ability to nail a parallel park, first pop. I'd look over my shoulder and instinctively know the angle I needed to take in order to park successfully. Then we bought a car with backing cameras. Now I had all this new information coming at me. For the first time in my life, I stopped relying on my gut and started to truly overthink my parallel park. A pattern began to emerge. The more I relied on the backing cameras, the more attempts I needed to nail the park. The more I did this, the more I focused on what a failure I was at parking. One day I decided enough was enough. I remembered how, for years, I had successfully parallel parked by looking over my shoulder. Ignoring the cameras, my past failures and the judgement oozing from the front seat passenger, I looked over my shoulder and relied on my intuition to successfully park on the first attempt.

While it is important that the decisions we make as a leader are aligned with our identity, it is not the only thing we should be relying on. In addition to our values and declarations, we should also be relying on input from others, wise counsel from those we trust, and successful past practices. But above all else, we need to trust ourselves.

BOUNDARIES

Having looked at how to use values to craft our identity as a leader and how this then enables us to make wise decisions, we are now going to explore the setting and keeping of boundaries. How boundaries are set varies from person to person. Even once set, they might change in response to the different situations we encounter. Regardless of the different circumstances that might influence our boundaries, what is important is that they are aligned with our personal values.

Underpinning our decisions with our values enables us to set and keep boundaries, irrespective of how we are feeling at the time. We've all been in situations where we've agreed to do something which, later on, we wished we hadn't. It is also easier to say no to something when we know that saying yes takes us away from our purpose and the identity we are crafting as a leader.

One of the things that can greatly influence people's boundaries is their disposition towards change. Some people can't wait to engage with change. They love exploring emerging ideas and coming up with fresh ways of doing things. They will push the boundaries of what is accepted practice and take risks that others wouldn't contemplate. At the other end of this spectrum are people who prefer the status quo. Their boundary wall, reflective of Fort Knox, is immediately erected in response to anything with the potential to disrupt. Boundaries around change are greatly influenced by where people sit on the Curve of Adoption.[22]

The Curve of Adoption is a useful measure to explain the different responses people have to new ideas or ways of doing things. Some people sit at the very front of the adoption curve. They are Innovators and Early Adopters. The majority sit in the middle of the curve. At the back sit the Laggards, the ones who find change challenging.

Healthy organisations are continuously growing and changing. They are usually led by people who encourage fresh ideas and new ways of doing things. Whether we are one of the first people to pick up and run with an idea or the last, it is important to know our natural place on the adoption curve, as this greatly influences the boundaries we set. Every group represented on the curve of adoption is important.

To help us understand each group within the curve, I'd like you to imagine there are 100 people in a room. In one corner sit two people who spend their lives inventing things. These are Innovators; people who are passionate about coming up with new ideas. Sitting close to the Innovators are 14 Early Adopters who love to peek over the Innovators' shoulders to get a glimpse of a potential future. These Early Adopters are visionaries; the dreamers who take the Innovators' ideas and come up with lots of different ways to use them. They like to take risks, and they enjoy the limelight which comes with being first.

In the centre of the room are 68 people who make up the majority. They are split into two groups. The first group is the Early Majority. They are people who love to make progress that is incremental and predictable. They only engage in new ideas if someone can show them how they will improve their lives or the lives of others. The second group in the centre of the room is the Late Majority. These people pride themselves on being conservative. They hold tightly to existing systems and play an important role in keeping the past and traditions alive. The Late Majority will embrace a new idea once the Early Majority are all doing it.

The last group of 16 people sit at the back of the room. They are the Laggards, who approach anything new with great scepticism.

Whilst they can be truly frustrating to leaders who are trying to drive an organisation forward, they are incredibly valuable because they are not scared to tell their truth. They are the children in the story of *The Emperor's New Clothes*, who, after the rest of the kingdom has already accepted his new wardrobe, point out that the emperor is not actually wearing anything.

Visualising yourself in this room, where do you think you would sit? Remember: every part of the adoption curve is important to an organisation. The Innovators keep the new ideas flowing, with the Early Adopters coming up with ways to capitalise on these and figure out how to make them useful. The Early Majority embed the ideas, with the Late Majority setting the pace of organisational change, ensuring the "baby isn't being thrown out with the bath water." Finally, the Laggards keep it real, and are a great asset when it comes to managing risk.

We will investigate the Curve of Adoption more when we dive into *Packing Cell Three: Setting Your Organisation Up for Success*, as it is important for leaders to understand how to manage each group on the journey of change. But for now, it is most important to know where we, personally, sit so that we can use this knowledge when setting our own boundaries. For example, people who are part of the Late Majority will have a completely different boundary around change than an Early Adopter. Likewise, Innovators shouldn't be surprised that people who are Laggards hold them at arm's length. However, this should never stop them from inventing.

As we become more experienced and successful as a leader, there will be a greater number of opportunities and expectations people will have for us. Knowing what to say yes to and, just as importantly, when to say no, is critical. Here is a decision tree that I have created that illustrates a process for figuring out boundaries.

Decisions, Boundaries, and Habits

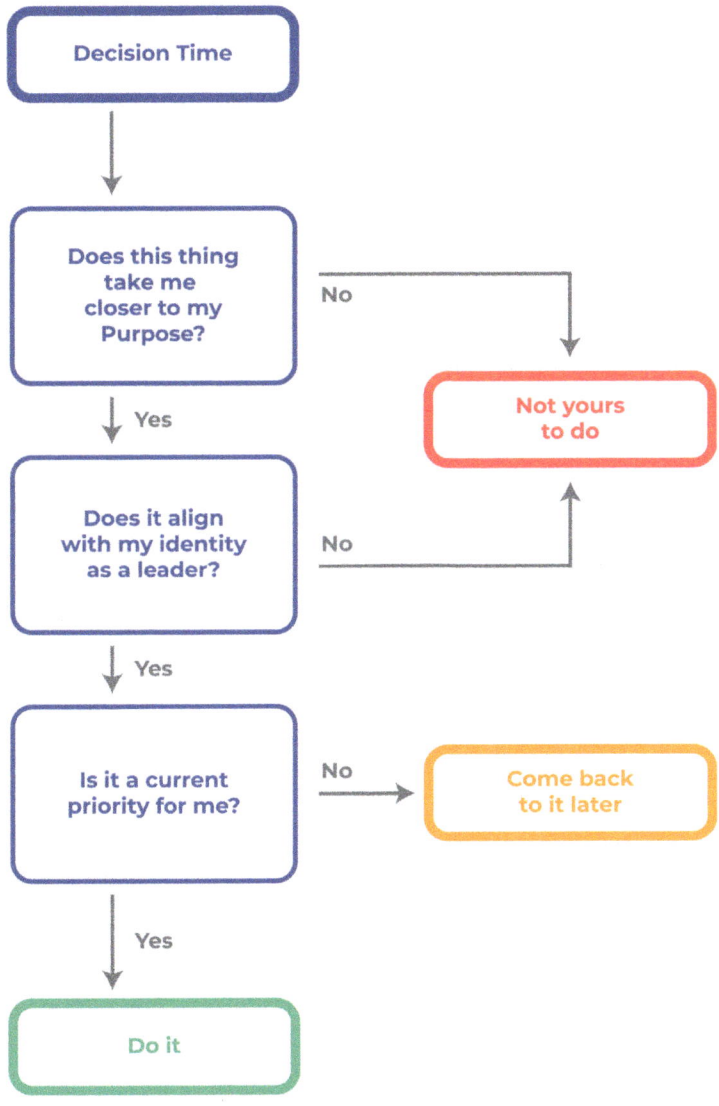

Figure 4.1
Boundary Decision Tree

The process starts with a decision about an opportunity or an expectation. The first thing to decide is if this has the potential to take us closer to our purpose or not. Obviously, if it takes us away from our purpose, then we will say no and leave it for someone else to do.

If the opportunity or expectation does take us closer to our purpose, then the next thing to decide is whether it fits with the identity we are crafting as a leader. For example, the opportunity might be a staff incentive programme, designed to increase the rate at which people come on board with the vision. This sounds like a great opportunity, but if our identity as a leader is that we want people to come on board because they are intrinsically motivated towards the vision, then this opportunity is not for us. Whilst it may not be right for us, for another leader with a different identity, it could well be the thing to which they say yes.

Assuming the opportunity or expectation is moving us closer to our purpose, and is aligned with our identity as a leader, then the final thing to decide is whether or not it is the right timing for us. This is where the Curve of Adoption comes into play. If we are a Late Majority leader and the opportunity is still sitting at the ideas stage, then whilst the opportunity might be right, the timing is wrong. If, however, this opportunity has been adopted by everyone else, then as a Late Majority, it will have become a priority. The right timing around a decision is as important as the decision itself.

Even though saying no can be difficult, there is often much greater opportunity on the other side of "no."

When I first started my design thinking and leadership practice, I was offered a three-day-a-week job. It ticked the box in terms of my 'equipping others for success' purpose, and had space for me to act in line with my identity as a leader. It would also give me a regular income at a time when I was still trying to figure out how I would make money out of my new venture. What it didn't satisfy was my place on the Curve of

Adoption. I'm an Early Adopter, and I am hugely energised by figuring out how to take new ideas and bring them to life. This was a well-established organisation, and I sensed at the interview that most of the role was about revamping the existing strategy. In the end, I turned it down, and I am so glad I did because not long after this, my business really started to take off.

Whenever we say yes to something, we are also saying no to something else. If I'd said yes to the job above, then I would have been saying no to a thriving design thinking and leadership practice. It is also salient to remember that once we've said yes to something, backtracking to a no is really, really difficult.

I find it helpful to say no slowly when I am turning opportunities down or declining to meet other people's expectations. This is a tried-and-true strategy, regularly employed by governments to prepare us for significant announcements. They do it by leaking small tidbits of information to the media. It is done so well, that the actual announcement, when it is finally made, is what everyone is expecting to hear. We can prepare people for our "no" as well. Sometimes it is as simple as asking: "Can I have a think and get back to you?" Then, when we get back to them, they will assume careful consideration has been given before the "no." Another strategy is to ask to discuss the implications of a decision with others before giving an answer. This delivers two benefits. Firstly, it helps the other person see that there is a possibility it isn't going to work, and secondly, it shows that the idea is being taken seriously. I find these strategies useful because they allow us to say no in a way that keeps the dignity of the other person intact. If we are serious about becoming a positive deviant, then we need to be committed to making and keeping our boundaries.

> *"Boundaries define us. They define what is me and what is not me. A boundary shows me where I end, and someone else begins, leading me to a sense of ownership. Knowing what I am to own and take responsibility for gives me freedom."*
> *- Henry Cloud & John Townsend[23]*

HABITS

Decisions and boundaries that enact our personal values are helpful, but it is when these become habits that we are truly set up for success as a leader.

> *"Habits: A routine or practice performed regularly; an automatic response to a specific situation."*
> *- James Clear[24]*

Habits are formed in the basal ganglia structures of our brain.[25] There are two phases of habit formation. Firstly, they are *associative*, which is the conscious association of action with a specific situation. For example, if part of our identity as a leader is to be fully present in conversations, then the action we might consciously take is to place our cell phone face down on the desk before embarking on a conversation. The action taken removes a potential distraction; the specific situation is being fully present when speaking to another person. The second phase of habit formation is *automatic*. This is when the learning that has occurred during the associative phase becomes part of a repertoire of stored habits that are applied automatically.

Sometimes we are not even aware that a habit has moved from

associative to automatic. This is a significant step in our journey towards positive deviance. For example, for years I had been deliberate about finding and then focussing on the "glass half full" interpretation of the things that were happening to me and the people around me. It was my conscious go-to strategy to manage any events that had the potential to negatively impact me, and those I led. I don't remember when this "re-focusing to the positive" habit moved from associative to automatic, but when my mother unexpectedly died, I became acutely aware of my now-automatic habit of finding the positive, even in the direst situations. Immediately following her death, I caught myself thinking about how grateful I was that she hadn't suffered, how much she would have hated being dependent on others for her needs, and how great it was that all her grandchildren made it to the hospital before she passed away. Even though I have no idea when this reframing habit became an automatic response, I was certainly grateful for it in the days following Mum's death. We explore this reframing more in Chapter Seven when we look at happiness and positive emotions.

All habits start as associative and are the conscious association of action with a specific situation. For a positive deviant, a specific situation is any time we enact a values-informed declaration to ensure our response aligns with the leader we are aspiring to be. This is not always easy. Many times, especially in my early years of leadership, I needed to exercise great self-control not to say what it was I really wanted to say. Instead, I would take a deep breath, draw on one of my declarations, and respond in a way that aligned with my values and my identity as the leader I was becoming. This is the crux of leaders being made, not born. We may possess a natural inclination towards leadership, but it is the work we do on ourselves, especially in the area of response management, that makes us the leader we aspire to be.

The journey of a habit moving from associative to automatic follows the exponential curve, as shown in Figure 4.2.

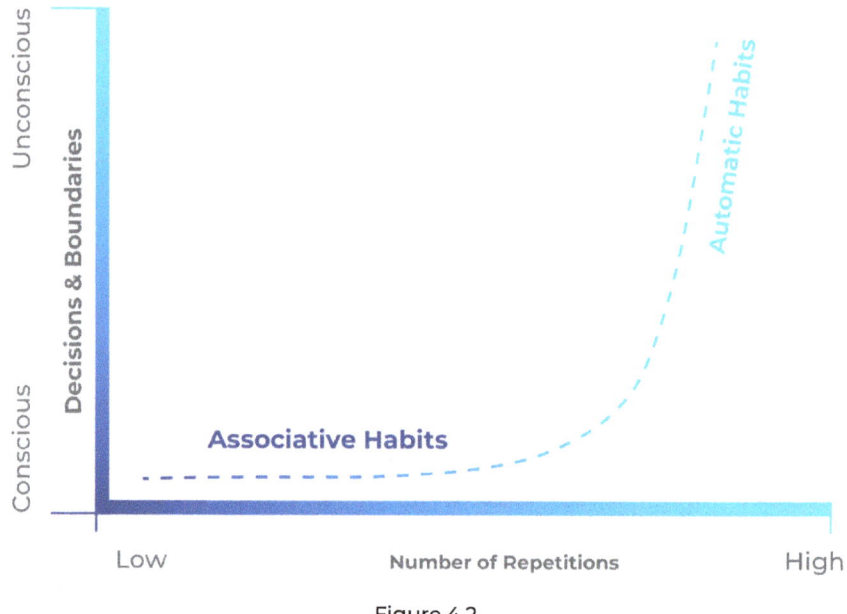

Figure 4.2
Exponential Nature of Habit Formation

At first, making decisions and boundaries that align with the leader we aspire to be, is a conscious endeavour. The more times we respond in our desired way, the closer we get to being able to do this unconsciously. But, like anything that follows an exponential curve, at first it feels like little progress is being made. Habits grow in a similar way to compound interest. At first, it will feel like you are not making progress. But if you consistently work hard to be the leader you aspire to be, then as James Clear, in his book *Atomic Habits*, says:

> *"Changes that seem small and unimportant at first will compound into remarkable results if you're willing to stick with them for years."*
> *– James Clear*[26]

Over time, the compounding effect of responding in alignment with our chosen identity as a leader will move a habit from associative to automatic. This is why it is so important to have our declarations in a prominent place: so that we are constantly reminded of the leader we are aspiring to be.

Then, one day we realise we are no longer aspiring to be that leader; we have become that leader. Remember my story from when I was a young leader, driving to a meeting where I planned to respond to a challenging situation, repeating my declaration about being a bridge builder over and over again? I never need to use this declaration now, as building bridges with people is an automatic habit and deeply embedded in who I am as a leader.

Building an automatic habit is the fastest way to positively deviate from your current responses. When we first step into a leadership role, we need to be very aware that the decisions we make and the boundaries we set will determine how others perceive us as leaders. A reputation, once established, is hard to change, so it is important to establish a good reputation from the outset.

Over time, as our boundaries and decisions become automatic habits, we come to the realisation that we are becoming the leader we aspire to be, through living a life aligned with our values. Most times, this is also the leader that our organisation needs us to be. The compounding effect of habits, no matter how small, is what leads to a thriving life.

> *"Success is the sum of small efforts*
> *– repeated day in and day out."*
> *– Robert Collier*

CHAPTER SUMMARY
Decisions, Boundaries, and Habits

Being clear about the identity of the leader we aspire to be enables us to respond to situations authentically and in a way that is aligned with how we want others to experience our leadership. Keeping our purpose, values and declarations at the centre of our decision-making is important for consistency and leads to high relational trust.

When making decisions, it is important to make space for the input of others, to listen to the counsel of those we trust, to be informed but not tied to practices of the past and to trust ourselves.

This chapter explored how we use our declarations to underpin our decision-making and to make and keep boundaries. We use three measures when setting boundaries:

1. Does this take me closer to my purpose?
2. Does it align with my identity as a leader?
3. Is it a current priority for me?

Over time consistent decision-making and boundary-holding grow into the habits that set us up to experience the thriving life of a positive deviant. There are two phases to habit formation, associative and automatic.

Forming habits around the identity we hold as a leader moves us closer to the leader we aspire to be, and the leader others need us to be. The compounding effect of habits, no matter how small, is what leads to a thriving life.

FROM IDEAS TO ACTION

- Over the course of a week, schedule a time each day to reflect on the key decisions you made, or boundaries you either kept or let slip.

- If you wrote yourself some leadership declarations after reading Chapter Three, can you identify the role they played in helping you make decisions or keep boundaries? If not, do they need to be tweaked or added to?

- Jot down some habits that you have developed over time. You might want to categorise these into habits that are helping you and ones that are not. How might you use your leadership declarations to overcome habits that aren't helping you? How might you use your leadership declarations to move your helpful habits from associative to automatic?

- Are there habits you see in others that you wish you had in your own life? Can you align them with your personal values? What decisions would you need to make and/or boundaries to keep in order to see this habit become part of your life?

5.
Strategies for Success

"Success is a state of mind. If you want success,
start thinking of yourself as a success."
- Joyce Brothers

Having explored the two innermost Circles of Positive Deviance, we now move to the third. This outer circle contains a range of strategies, all drawn from the field of positive psychology, that set us up to thrive and not just survive.

Understanding how our personal values, habits, decisions and boundaries help us develop our identity as a leader is important, but it is not enough. To be fully equipped for a life of positive deviance, we need a range of specific strategies we can employ. The outer Circle of Positive Deviance gives us these strategies (Figure 5.1).

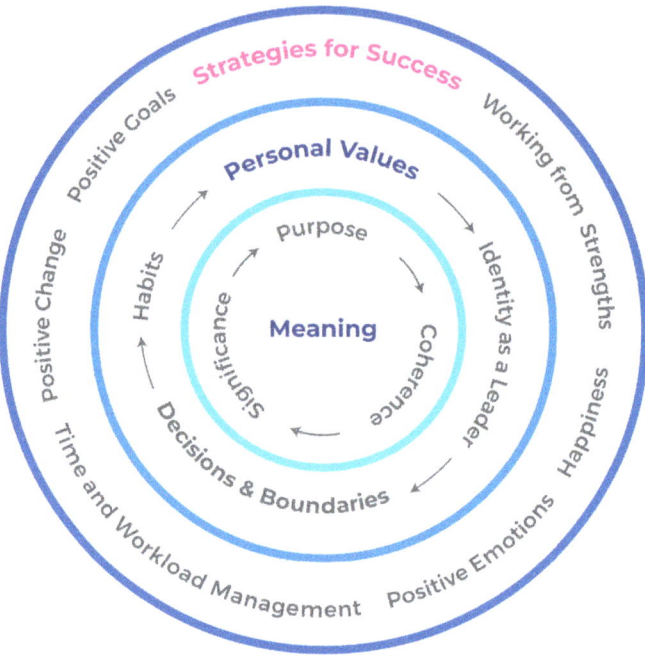

Figure 5.1
Circles of Positive Deviance

We can't always control what happens to us, but we can control how we respond. The strategies contained in the outer Circle of Positive Deviance teach us the responses that will help us to thrive despite the circumstance. No matter what happens to us, we get to choose whether we stand back and let others write our stories, or lean in and write the stories for ourselves.

The strategies for success contained in the final part of this book are like superpowers for positive deviants. They are all strategies I use to ensure that I thrive and not just survive. No matter what life throws at us we still get to choose how we will respond, as illustrated in the following story.

When my younger brother was diagnosed with acute myeloid leukaemia at age 29, my husband and I consciously made the decision that whatever happened, we would be a better-not-bitter family as a result of this devastating situation. Our children, at the time, were aged 12 and 10, and it was really important for us to support them positively as we navigated a situation no family ever wants to find themselves in.

As soon as my brother was diagnosed, the search for a bone marrow donor began. Both my sister and I were compatible, but I was the one chosen as the most suitable. Initially, I really struggled with being the donor. There was no way I wasn't going to do it, but I was wracked with guilt, because I didn't actually want to do it. I struggled with reconciling how I could love someone but feel so negatively about suffering on their behalf. Then, one Sunday morning in the midst of my grappling, the sermon at church was all about love. The minister talked about enduring love as being something you do, rather than something you feel. This realisation not only changed my attitude towards making a bone marrow donation, but it forever changed my perspective about love. I was able to reframe my thinking about the bone marrow donation to being something I did because I loved my brother, not because of any feeling I might or might not have.

The bone marrow transplant was successful, but sadly the leukaemia returned, and this time despite my sister donating her platelets, my brother died just shy of his 33rd birthday.

Thinking back about this time, I know I did become a better person. Journeying through this situation taught me about the power of reframing situations, no matter how bad, to the positive.

I didn't know it at the time, but all of the trauma that surrounded my brother's illness and death was what started me on my positive deviant journey.[27] I realised that no matter what I was going through, I could respond in a way that would leave me as a better, not bitter, person.

An important thing to understand as we dive into these strategies, is that as humans, we all have a negative bias. This means we attend more closely to negative things than positive ones, and it is probably a hangover from the days when humans were hunters and gatherers. During this time our forebears had to pay close attention to potential risks in order to survive. Chapter One of this book explored our modern-day survival responses: fight, flight, freeze, and fawn. I believe these are still our default positions, which means that every day, we have the opportunity to control our negative bias by choosing to positively deviate from it.

The rest of this chapter gives an overview of each of the strategies for success that, over time, will transform us into positive deviants. I have listed them in the order I think they are best deployed, starting with "Working from Strengths", and moving around the Circles of Deviance clockwise, to finish with "Positive Goals." Each strategy can be deployed individually or combined with other strategies. You may notice that some strategies which appear separately in the Circles of Deviance are combined with others in the same chapter. This has been done to illustrate the symbiotic relationship between some strategies (for example, positive change and positive goals). Some strategies may become your 'modus operandi,' while others will be strategies you employ when and as you need them.

WORKING FROM STRENGTHS

Thinking about how we might work more from our strengths is our first strategy for success. For too long, we have focussed on trying to fix our weaknesses, rather than amplifying our strengths. Professional growth plans are littered with goals designed to fix the things we are not so good at, rather than encouraging the growth of the things we do well. This is not to say we shouldn't be working to improve ourselves. It's quite the opposite. This is about improving ourselves by becoming aware of our strengths. Using a positive psychology lens, we are able to explore how we can shape our lives and, in particular, our jobs to do more of what we are good at.

HAPPINESS AND POSITIVE EMOTIONS

Our second strategy for success explores happiness and positive emotions. Our negative bias means that we feel negative emotions more intensely and respond more powerfully to negative events. For example, we recall negative feedback comments more readily than positive ones. It is truly human to run away from the negative, but only walk towards the positive.

Our happiness can be deeply affected by our negative bias. But the good news is that we can do something about it. As humans, we experience both negative and positive emotions. When we alter our thinking to focus on the positive aspects of situations, this increases the positive emotions we feel which in turn increases our happiness. Learning how to run towards the positive is a key behaviour used by positive deviants to increase the amount of happiness they experience in their lives.

TIME AND WORKLOAD MANAGEMENT

Managing our time and workload is a key strategy for success. Often people complain about an excessive workload ahead of understanding how they make use of their time. In Chapter Eight, we explore in-depth the relationship between time and workload.

As humans, we are often good at making a job fit into the time available. I'm often asked how long it takes me to write my weekly blog. The answer is it depends on how much time I have. If I have a whole day, it will take a day; if I only have an hour, you'd be amazed at how fast I can write! Once we have a good understanding of how we use our time, then we are in a position to decide whether we are managing a reasonable or unreasonable workload.

POSITIVE CHANGE AND POSITIVE GOALS

The final strategies for success are positive change and positive goals. We look at the two ways positive change occurs: there is change that is happening to us, and there is change we initiate and drive. We look at how the timing of new initiatives impacts momentum around both personal and professional change.

We also look at goal-setting, which we know can be a key element to successful change processes. We look at the different types of goals we can set and what constitutes a positive goal. We also look at how to set positive goals and the conditions that greatly increase the likelihood of us achieving them.

POSITIVE DEVIANCE AND FALSE POSITIVITY

The strategies for success that have been outlined above are based on research from the field of positive psychology. They are strategies that have turned me into a positive deviant and ones that I hope others will find helpful as well. Before going on to look at these strategies in more depth, I want to stress that practising positive deviance is not living a life of false positivity. Sometimes referred to as toxic positivity, it is a deceitful practice that, over time, has the potential to completely derail us. The difference between positive deviance and false positivity is exemplified in Jim Collins'[28] *Stockdale Paradox*.

The Stockdale Paradox is named after Admiral Jim Stockdale, who survived eight years in a prisoner-of-war camp during the Vietnam War. During an interview, Collins asked him what it was that caused him to survive. Stockdale replied that you needed two things. Firstly, an unwavering faith that you'll prevail in the end, and secondly, the discipline to confront the brutal facts. Collins also asked him who didn't make it out. Stockdale replied that it was the optimists. They were the ones who'd say "We'll be out by Christmas" and then Christmas came and went and they were still imprisoned. This latter response is a powerful example of false positivity.

My brother died two weeks before my 40th birthday. In the months leading up to my birthday, I had been fretting about being that old. I'd mercilessly teased my friends about being over the hill when they turned 40, and now it was coming up to be my turn. As another example of reframing situations to the positive, after my brother died at 32, I knew that I could no longer think negatively about birthdays. Turning 40 meant I'd had just over seven more years of life than my brother had. Ever since that time, I've celebrated being alive on each birthday rather than dwelling on the fact I'm getting older.

Each of the following chapters explores in depth a strategy you can apply to your life to help you reset your bias from negative to positive. As you work through the chapters, be brave enough to confront your brutal reality, while at the same time holding faith that you will prevail to the end.

CHAPTER SUMMARY
Strategies for Success

Knowing why we lead and how we lead is not enough. We also need specific strategies in order to thrive every day.

We can't always control the things that happen in our life, but we can control our responses.

Increasing our focus on the positive is the way to address our negative bias, and the key to positive deviance.

The Stockdale Paradox teaches us to retain unwavering faith while confronting the brutal facts.

FROM IDEAS TO ACTION

- Can you identify specific things that are currently happening to you that you'd love to positively deviate away from? What are they? Which of the strategies mentioned in this chapter might help?

- Can you pinpoint areas of your life that are more vulnerable to a negative bias? Are you able to identify why this might be? Are you able to come up with a plan to increase the positivity in these situations?

- Is there a situation you are currently navigating that needs the Stockdale Paradox applied to it in order for you to eventually succeed?

6.
Working from Strengths

*"Strengths: a pre-existing capacity for a particular way of
behaving, thinking or feeling that is authentic
and energising to the user and enables optimal functioning,
development and performance."*
- Alex Linley

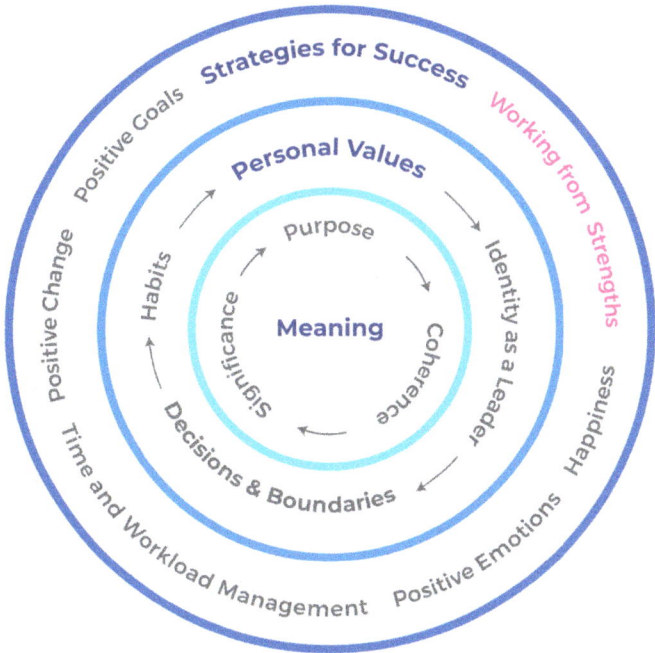

Figure 6.1
Circles of Positive Deviance

Research from the field of positive psychology has found that people who know, understand, and work from their strengths, are more resilient, happier, and energised. They experience less stress, and are more likely to achieve their goals. The research also tells us that taking a strengths-approach to our work lets us build on what it is we do well, and increases our potential.[29,30,31,32]

Working from a place of strength is also the best way to circumvent our weaknesses.[33] For example, I am weak at explaining my ideas by drawing them. However, I have a strength in writing, and so it is probably no surprise that if I want to explain an idea, I will write about, rather than draw it. On occasion, I have tried to improve upon my drawing skills, but unless I want to be a better visual artist, this is not a productive use of time. I know that no matter how much work I do to improve my drawing skills, I'm never going to become as skilled at drawing as I am at writing. I instead focus on accomplishing what I need done through my strength.

In order to work from our strengths, there are three things we need to do:

1. Become consciously **aware** of our strengths.
2. Take time to **explore** our strengths, so that we fully understand how they play out in our lives.
3. Know how best to **apply** our strengths, in order to set ourselves up for success.

This *Aware, Explore and Apply* model comes from the VIA Institute on Character and is a simple, yet effective framework with which to engage with strengths.[34] We feel engaged and energised when we know and are in a position to grow our strengths.

AWARE

The first step to working from strengths is to be aware of our own strengths. There are lots of ways to do this. We can do some strengths-spotting on ourselves. Some ideas for this are:

- Write a list of all the things you enjoy doing.
- Notice what you are doing when you feel most energised.
- Identify what you do when you are at your best.
- Observe what you talk about that always gets you excited.
- Write a list of the tasks you find easy. Identify the common elements of these tasks.
- Notice the sorts of things you find easy to learn.
- Think back to your childhood and identify anything you did then, that you still do now.

We can also ask others about the strengths they spot in us. Some of the questions you might ask them are:

- What do they see you doing when you are at your best?
- How would they describe you to a stranger?
- What is something they always trust you to get right?

Another strategy to uncover strengths is to take an online assessment. The *VIA Character Strengths Survey*[35] is a free assessment that provides you with your top 24 character strengths. Of the paid assessments, *Cliftons and Strengths Profile Assessments* would be the most well-known. My personal favourite is the *Strengths Profile Assessment,* which was designed by Alex Linley, the founding director of The Centre for Applied Positive Psychology. A *Strengths*

Profile Assessment is different from other strengths assessments, because it assesses energy and the contexts in which we use our strengths. This enables us to know which strengths not only work best for us, but also leave us feeling energised.

> *"Simply put, strengths energise people enabling them to be at their best."*
> - Alex Linley[36]

EXPLORE

Once you've become aware of your strengths, it is important that you analyse your results so you can begin to understand how the strengths play out in your life. This is important for two reasons. Firstly, a debrief of your results maximises the impact of the assessment. In fact, there is research evidence that points to a higher likelihood that people who participate in a strengths debrief are more likely to take action, based on what they discover.[37] Secondly, an assessment debrief is important to prevent you from misinterpreting your results, which could leave you in a worse-off position.

If you have used the VIA free assessment, they have resources on their website to help you with this. You might also share your assessment with people who know you well and talk with them about how aligned your results are with how they perceive your strengths. Finally, some people find it useful to reflect on their day through the lens of their strengths, identifying when they have made use of their specific strengths.

If you decide to pay for an assessment, it'd be best to organise this through a qualified strength coach. Generally, you pay one fee that gives you access to the assessment and a one-hour debrief. Strength coaches can provide clarity around each strength profile. Some strengths, such as Connector and Rapport Builder, may seem similar. But, when we delve into what they mean in the assessment, we see they are quite different. For example, Connector is about making connections between people, whereas Rapport Builder is about quickly establishing rapport and relationships with others. The strengths debrief also helps people understand the different parts of an assessment and the best way to engage with them. This makes it easier for people to regularly re-visit their reports to gain further insights.

APPLY

After taking the time to become aware of and explore our strengths, we are now ready to apply them to our work. Our most useful strengths have three things in common. They are the ones we perform well, are energised by and use a lot.[38] Combining these three aspects, performance, energy and use, enables us to identify the best strengths from which to work. It is also useful to understand how to manage strengths that only tick some of the boxes. This is illustrated in Figure 6.2.

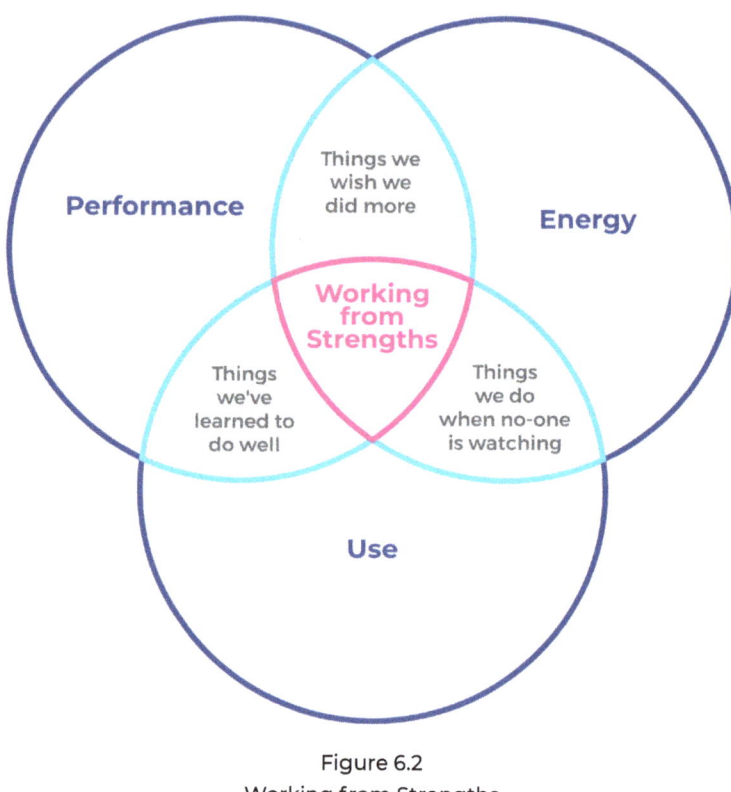

Figure 6.2
Working from Strengths

Performance + Use + Energy = Working From Strengths

Strengths that we perform well, use frequently, and are energised by, are the key strengths we should be working from whenever possible. As mentioned previously, I have strength in writing. I am told by others that I write well (performance), I do a lot of writing every week (use), and I am invigorated by the process (energy). I use my writing strength in different ways. At one end of my 'use' spectrum is the blog I write every week which is read by over a thousand people. At the other end is my workshop superpower: I can listen to a whole lot of dialogue around a topic and then go to the whiteboard and summarise what the room is saying, in one or two succinct statements.

Performance + Energy = Things We Wish We Did More

These are strengths we perform well and are energised by, but for varied reasons, we don't get to use them as often as we might like. For example, curiosity is one of my strengths. I've always been someone who asks a lot of questions. I am especially curious about history, so it is no surprise that I love spending time in museums. Unfortunately, it is only during the holidays that I am able to use my curiosity strength and visit museums.

Performance + Use = Things We've Learned To Do Well

There are things we have learnt to do well, but we are not energised by. For example, listening is an important leadership strength. For some leaders, listening to others comes naturally; for others it is something they have had to learn to do. For this latter group of leaders, spending their day listening to others, whilst important to their role, can be quite draining. This is an example of something they have learned to do but are de-energised by. If we spend too much of our day doing things that sap our energy, we can be left feeling stressed and unmotivated. In the example above, being de-energised by listening is not an excuse to not listen; it is, however, an opportunity to think about how to structure the way we work so that we can intersperse the activities that we know drain us, with activities that we find invigorating.

Another way to manage the parts of our roles that de-energise us is to use our strengths to counter them. For example, one of my learned behaviours is personal responsibility. This means that I have a strong bias towards taking care of things by myself. What this looks like, is that I struggle to ask others for help even when I am under pressure. I can use my realised strength of enabler to counter my learned behaviour of personal responsibility. By drawing on my enabler strength, asking for help becomes easy, as I am now seeing it as helping others to feel fulfilled and to grow.

Spending too much of our time doing things that de-energise is a bit like not getting enough sleep. We can get away with it for periods of time, but in the long run, it will always catch up with us.

Energy + Use = Things We Do When No One Is Watching

These are the things we do because we enjoy them, but we are not necessarily good at them. If we can't sing in tune and we know it, then we will probably only sing in places when we don't have an audience. An exception to this might be at a karaoke bar after one or two drinks too many. It is possible to energetically do something we enjoy but are not good at. Some people sing in the shower or dance to *Mama Mia* with the curtains closed. There are very few times that others see us in this space.

Applying our strengths

While it is undoubtedly useful to understand our strengths, we need to be mindful of how and when we apply them. There are four key things to consider when leading through our strengths:

1. Be careful to not overuse strengths

For example, detail is one of my top strengths. I see things that others might miss. I am also in danger of over-using this strength when I explain something. I have to keep reminding myself that too much detail is as bad as too little.

2. Be willing to step out of your comfort zone to make better use of under-utilised strengths

Humour was a strength I discovered that I was not utilising enough. I think I was scared that if I was funny, people wouldn't take me seriously. As I started to step out of my comfort zone and bring more humour to my work, I realised that people didn't take me less seriously and that using humour brought a new energy to my work. I now use humour as a deliberate strategy to lift the energy in a room when it is flagging.

3. Balance activities that deplete your energy with things that energise you

Manage your calendar in such a way that you intersperse your energy-sapping activities with things that invigorate you. If you are de-energised by writing, but energised by talking with people, schedule a catch-up with someone to follow a focussed period of writing.

4. Work around your weaknesses in preference to trying to 'fix them"

Too often areas of weakness become the focus for professional development. If it is at all possible, delegate tasks that require you to work from an area of weakness to someone who has a strength in that area. If this is not possible, try to find a strength you can work through instead of your weakness. For example, if you loathe speaking in public, but have a strength in writing, ask to be able to present your ideas in writing instead of having to present them to a room full of people.

> *"Strengths are so integral to our identity as individuals and as human beings. They are at the heart of what it takes to lead flourishing lives."*
> *- Alex Linley*

Being aware of, exploring, and applying our strengths allows us to be more strategic in how we carry out our day-to-day work. Shaping the way we work allows us to spend more time in an energised space and ensures we work in a way that others appreciate. Working from strengths greatly increases our chances of living a meaningful life that is aligned with our values. When we understand our strengths, we are able to be deliberate in the way we operate, which sets us up for success as a leader.

CHAPTER SUMMARY
Working from Strengths

People who know, understand, and work from their strengths experience less stress, are more resilient, happier, energised and more likely to achieve their goals.

Taking a strengths approach to our work lets us build on what it is we do well, increasing our potential.

Aware, *Explore* and *Apply* is a useful framework through which to utilise our strengths.

There are many ways to identify our strengths, from strengths spotting to online assessments.

It is important to spend time analysing our strengths as this increases our chances of taking action, based on what we discover.

When we understand our strengths, we are able to be deliberate in the way we operate which sets us up for success as a leader.

FROM IDEAS TO ACTION

- What do you see as your greatest strengths? How do these help you succeed?

- Are you able to identify any situations when your strengths might actually be starting to play against you?

- What strengths do you have that perhaps you could be making more use of? What would you need to do differently in order for this to happen?

7.
Happiness and Positive Emotions

"I am determined to be cheerful and happy in whatever situation I may find myself. For I have learned that the greater part of our misery or unhappiness is determined not by our circumstances but by our disposition."
- Martha Washington

Figure 7.1
Circles of Positive Deviance

Happiness and positive emotions are two different Strategies for Success that have a symbiotic relationship. We feel happy when we are experiencing positive emotions, and we are more likely to feel positive emotions when we are doing or experiencing something that makes us happy. The combination of happiness and positive emotions gives us the sense that our life is good.

At times being a leader can be challenging. We can make it less so if we develop habits that increase the amount of happiness we experience in our roles; for example, taking time each day to acknowledge what has gone well, and to pause and enjoy moments of breakthrough. Leaders are often on the receiving end of negative criticism. To sustain ourselves as leaders, we need strategies that help us to counter the negative emotions that come from this criticism with positive emotions. Leaders who are happy have a tendency to infect those around them with increased levels of positivity.

HAPPINESS

Have you ever noticed that some people are naturally happier than others? If you have, then you are correct. We all have a set point that determines our predisposition for happiness.[39] People with a high set point are generally happy, while those with a low one are mostly unhappy. Researchers, through the study of fraternal and identical twins, have shown that our set point for happiness is based on our genetics.[40] For better or worse, our set point for happiness is pretty much fixed for life. The positive side of this is that when we go through dark seasons, eventually, we will regain our equilibrium and return to the normalcy of our happiness set point.

Happiness and Positive Emotions

Unfortunately, a happiness set point also means that the impact of positive experiences does not last.

In recent years there has been a significant focus on well-being. Many organisations have invested in initiatives to increase the well-being experienced by their employees. Sadly, one-off events such as lunchtime speakers, or weekly group yoga sessions, do little to improve individual well-being. We're hardly home from the inspirational conference we have just attended before the reality of life hits us and our happiness returns to its set point.

Fortunately, we still have a chance to make an impact. Our happiness set point only determines 50% of our happiness. Our happiness is also impacted by life's experiences, which account for about 10%, and intentional activity, which accounts for the remaining 40%. Sonja Lyubomirsky[41] used a Happiness Pie to illustrate this, which is reproduced in Figure 7.2.

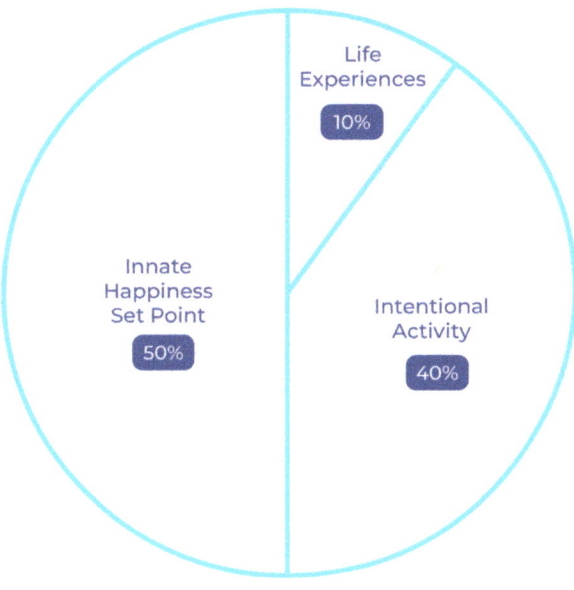

Figure 7.2
Lyubomirsky's (2017) Happiness Pie

This means that even if we are unlucky enough to be born with a low set point for happiness and life has thrown us lots of curve balls, influence over happiness is possible through a protracted intentional activity that is driven by the individual. Inspirational speakers and yoga do have a place in the well-being space, but only if individuals take what they have learnt and apply it to their lives on a regular basis.

> *"Despite the finding that our happiness is partially genetically influenced and despite the finding that our life situations have a surprisingly small impact on how happy we are, still a very large portion of happiness - up to 40% - is in our power to change."*
> *– Sonja Lyubomirsky*

We can be intentional about increasing our happiness. Here are some of the many intentional activities we can undertake to do this.

Gratitude

Gratitude can be either a spontaneous or deliberate practice. It is about noticing and appreciating the good things in life. It's also about not taking anyone or anything for granted. People who practise gratitude are also more likely to help others. Practising gratitude can also be healing after a traumatic experience; for example, moments after my mother's unexpected death, I was able to be grateful that she hadn't had to suffer, and that all her grandchildren had been able to visit her in hospital before she died.

Helping Others

We benefit most from helping others when we have no expectation of a reward for doing so. When we help others, we build connections, which can lead to a sense of belonging. Helping others improves our overall sense of purpose and identity.

Acts of Kindness

An act of kindness is when we go out of our way to do something for someone else without any expectation of a reward. Acts of kindness are underpinned by generosity, helpfulness, and an appreciation of other people's feelings.

Nurturing Social Relationships

When we nurture our social relationships, we build long-term authentic connections. Common ways to nurture social relationships are being fully present, spending time together, practising non-judgement, offering emotional support and showing appreciation.

Savouring Life's Pleasures

This is when we enjoy life's pleasures slowly in order to enjoy an experience as much as possible. We might savour in anticipation of a trip or an event; we might savour in the moment, pausing to celebrate a significant achievement; or we might savour through bringing to mind memories of past events that brought us much joy. For example, looking through a photo album from a trip.

BEING HAPPY IS IMPORTANT

> *"Happiness predicts success in nearly every life domain, from health and longevity to workplace and academic performance, creativity and relationships."*
> *- Lyubomirsky, King & Diener*[42]

Success as a leader can be defined in many ways. From the outside, it might be defined in terms of the role we hold or the amount we earn. But for me, success as a leader is best measured by the happiness I experience from knowing I am making a difference.

Being happy is important. Three researchers[43] from the field of positive psychology have found that happier people are healthier and live longer. Not only this, happy people are less accident-prone, more productive, and work harder. They are also more caring and socially engaged. Ironically, they are also more likely to consider themselves lucky, not realising that through living a happy life, they are creating their own luck.

Taking all of the above into account, we can see that being happy pays enormous dividends. People who live happy lives enjoy a better quality of life, have more friends, and have greater life satisfaction. It is no wonder that the most common thing parents say they want for their children is to be happy. If our lives are not as happy as we would like them to be, then it is certainly worth investing time in intentional activities that increase our happiness.

EUDAIMONIC AND HEDONIC HAPPINESS

Another important thing to know about happiness is that there are two types of happiness: eudaimonic and hedonic happiness. Eudaimonic happiness is the joy achieved through experiences of meaning and fulfilment. Hedonic happiness is the joy achieved through experiences of pleasure and enjoyment.

Eudaimonic happiness is rooted in meaning and purpose. It is the psychological well-being we get from deep relationships, personal growth, and a meaningful life. Eudaimonic happiness is characterised by living in accordance with our values. It is the joy we experience when we see the coherence between, and the significance of, our endeavours in relation to our purpose. It is the happiness we feel when we help others or engage in creative pursuits.

Eudaimonic happiness is what new parents and grandparents experience when the baby arrives; it is what a teacher experiences when a child who has been struggling, suddenly gets it. It is what a nurse experiences when they see a patient's condition begin to improve; it is what a sports coach experiences when their team wins. Eudaimonic happiness is different for every person but is rooted in finding purpose and fulfilment in our daily activities.

Hedonic happiness is a measure of our overall satisfaction with life and generally comes with high levels of positive emotions. We can probably all think of people whose lives are skewed towards hedonic happiness, full of pleasure and experience. But the challenge of hedonic happiness is its close relationship with positive change. The first time we experience a positive change, we experience high levels of positive emotion and happiness. I'll never forget the first time I was upgraded to business class on a long-haul flight: I'd never felt so happy on a plane, and I even wished the journey could be longer. After my fourth experience of business class, the initial surge of happiness was long gone and the luxurious flight was back to being a long-haul. This is an example of hedonic adaption. Once I was used to business class, it no longer gave me the happiness it once did. The positive emotions attached to hedonic happiness never last, which is what drives people to search for greater hedonic pleasures.

> *"Without meaning people fill
> the void with hedonic pleasures."*
> - Viktor E. Frankl

Without the balance of eudaimonic happiness, the trappings of hedonic happiness become meaningless. The shiny new things we crave, or the pleasures we pursue, no longer fill us with the joy they once did. We are driven to acquire more assets and experiences, yet never attain the happiness we seek.

This imbalance of happiness goes both ways. People who have careers in areas such as health and education probably choose this vocation because of the meaning and fulfilment it brings. To ensure longevity, people in these types of careers need to intentionally inject into their lives guilt-free hedonic happiness, to reduce their risk of burnout. It is also important for people in these roles to realise that not everyone is driven by eudaimonic happiness. True happiness comes from having a balance between meaning and purpose and experiences of pleasure and enjoyment.

To be truly happy, we need both eudaimonic and hedonic happiness in our lives. Positive deviants are able to balance these two happiness states as illustrated in Figure 7.3.

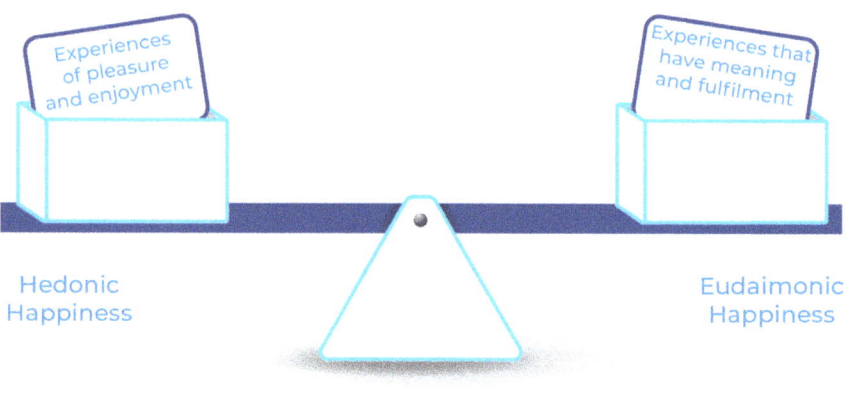

Figure 7.3
The Happiness Balance

"Probably the biggest insight ... is that happiness is not just a place but also a process ... Happiness is an ongoing process

of fresh challenges, and ... it takes the right attitude and activities to continue to be happy."
- Ed Diener

POSITIVE EMOTIONS

In 1996, neurologist Jill Bolte Taylor[44] had a massive stroke. Her recovery from this event greatly influenced her work as a neuro-anatomist. One of her key discoveries is what she calls her '90-second rule.'

> *"When a person has a reaction to something in their environment, there's a 90 second chemical process that happens; any remaining emotional response is just the person choosing to stay in that emotional loop."*[45]

This means that the length of time it takes our body to experience an emotion is 90 seconds. The experience of a negative emotion usually starts with an adrenaline rush, then our face heats up, our throat grows tight, and our heart races. This physiological response all happens in 90 seconds. What happens next, depends on what we do next.

Emotions are linked to our body and brain and therefore influence our behaviour. There are lots of things that drive behaviour - past experiences, the stories we tell ourselves, our values, beliefs, thoughts, and attitudes, to name but a few. It is our behavioural response that determines how long we will be impacted by the emotion once the 90 seconds are over. For example, if we think we have been treated unfairly we, in all likelihood, will experience negative emotions. If our unfair treatment is all we talk and think about for the rest of the day, then the impact from the negative emotion will continue to impact us well after the initial 90 seconds.

As humans, we are in the driving seat when it comes to our behaviour. Whilst at times we might make an unguarded response, the majority of times, we have full control over how we respond to situations. This is why the strategies in Chapter Three around using our values to craft our identity are so important. If we know the type of person we aspire to be, then we can use this knowledge when deciding how we are going to move forward once the 90-second negative emotion hit is over. More often than not, this is a deliberate choice, as illustrated in the following story:

My father suffers so badly from dementia, he is in full-time hospital care. The week he turned 85, I arranged my schedule so that I could fly down to be with the rest of my family for a small celebration. Our hope was that even though he no longer remembered what day of the week it was, let alone his birthday, familiar faces turning up with a cake and candle would give him a small amount of birthday joy.

While I waited for my flight, I started writing my weekly blog post. I'd chosen to write about the importance of keeping a glass-half-full attitude when responding to unwelcome events. I was in full writing flow when a ping on my phone alerted me to a flight delay, then another delay and then another one. I finally boarded the plane at the exact time the rest of the family was singing Happy Birthday to my father. I was devastated.

The irony of my blog post was not lost on me. I decided that the universe had given me a great opportunity to practise what I preach. So I sat on the plane, laptop on my knee, and struggling not to give into my tears, I forced myself to acknowledge that negative emotions only last 90 seconds. Now, I needed to act.

I began to list all the positive things that could come out of my disappointment. Some of these were:

"Visiting Dad after the rest of the family has left, will mean that he will spend more of his birthday filled with people he knows."

"My daughter will video the celebration so I will still see it. We will have a record we may not have thought to create otherwise."

"Dad has no concept of time, so me visiting him later will mean I get to tell him about the celebration his family organised for him."

The more I focussed on the positive things that could come out of this unlucky situation, the better I felt. It was a good reminder that we don't get to choose whether or not we will experience negative emotions (we will), but that we do get to choose how we will react once the 90 seconds are passed.

What we do immediately after we feel an emotion determines how long we are impacted by it. Dwelling on the circumstances that led to the emotion, both positive and negative, determines the level of unhappiness or happiness that we will experience. No one enjoys experiencing negative emotions, but it is important to understand that in the same way our bodies use experiences of pain to keep us safe (e.g. a hand on a hot stove element), our bodies use emotional pain to help us avoid making the same mistakes again and again. We only develop emotional resilience through emotional pain. Emotional resilience leads to a stronger sense of self, increased compassion, and a happier life.

GRATITUDE, SAVOURING AND OPTIMISM

We experience positive emotions in three key ways: gratitude, savouring and optimism. Gratitude is focusing on the good things that have happened to us. Some people keep a gratitude diary in which they record on a regular basis their positive experiences. Some people set aside specific time to recall and appreciate the good in their lives. The second key way to experience positive emotions is through savouring. This is when we pause to consciously attend to our experiences so that we savour the moment. It might be pausing on a bush walk to savour the sounds and smell of nature, or it might be to hold some delicious food in your mouth to reap the full benefit of the flavours. The third way we experience positive emotions is through optimism. This is when we choose to think about the future in terms of the best that could happen.

Some people categorise these three key ways to increase positive emotions by thinking about gratitude as past experiences, savouring as present moments, and optimism as future dreams. I think the reality is more nuanced than this, as illustrated in Figure 7.4.

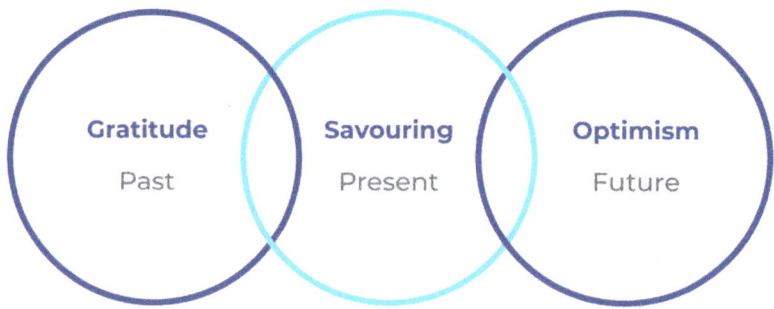

Figure 7.4
Three Key Ways to Experience Positive Emotions

While gratitude is mainly about creating positive emotions linked to the past, we also savour as we look back and remember past positive experiences. For example, I savour the memories of holidays past. Savouring mainly occurs in the present, although it does take a conscious effort to pause our busy lives and savour the moment. While we mainly link the future with optimism, we can also savour the expectation of experiences that are about to come. For example, a music fan savouring the expectation that comes with the experience of buying a ticket to see a favourite band play live. While we are able to savour by thinking about future events, optimism is what drives positive emotions when we think about the future in more general terms.

AMPLIFYING THE IMPACT OF POSITIVE EMOTIONS

In Chapter Four, we explored the use of our declarations about the leader we aspire to be as a tool to counter the impact of any negative emotions we may experience. Our declarations can also be useful to amplify the impact of positive emotions, as we savour the moments when we see our declarations become our lived reality.

The most common positive emotions we experience are:

- Joy
- Gratitude
- Serenity
- Interest
- Hope
- Pride
- Amusement

- Inspiration
- Awe
- Love

We don't all experience these emotions in equal measure. If there is one positive emotion we'd like to experience more of, then Barbara Fredrickson's "Hunt and Gather" exercise is a helpful way to do this.[46] This exercise gets people to use their phone cameras to take photos of the times they are experiencing the positive emotion that they want to experience more. These photos are then compiled into a portfolio that can be either digital or paper-based. People are then invited to regularly revisit these photos to remind themselves of the times when they experienced the specific positive emotion. This is an example of Fredrickson's "Broaden and Build Theory"; when we broaden our thought-action repertoire around a specific emotion, it causes us to build our intellectual or psychological response.[47]

Some people find it useful to choose one positive emotion on which to focus when creating a positive emotion portfolio.

Like a battery, we need both positive and negative emotions to keep us fully charged and working. As illustrated in Figure 7.5, it is helpful to think of a negative emotion as a call to action, whereas a positive emotion is a reward for taking proper action.

Happiness and Positive Emotions

Figure 7.5
Negative and Positive Emotional Responses

Both positive and negative emotions are important and have specific functions. Emotional intelligence is when we are managing our emotions rather than being managed by them. Positive deviants set themselves up for success by taking deliberate action to minimise the impact of negative emotions and amplify the impact of positive ones.

> *"The quality of your life is directly related to the quality of your emotions."*
> *- Sue Langley*

CHAPTER SUMMARY
Happiness and Positive Emotions

We feel happy when we are experiencing positive emotions.

We are born with a set point for happiness which determines 50% of how happy we are. Our life experiences account for 10%. The remaining 40% can be impacted through intentional activity.

Happy people enjoy many benefits and are generally more successful than unhappy people.

We can increase our happiness through practising gratitude, helping others, acts of kindness, building social relationships, and savouring life experiences. This happens through intentional and sustained practice.

Hedonic happiness is the joy achieved through experiences and pleasure, and eudaimonic happiness comes from experiences of meaning and fulfilment. It is important to balance these two types of happiness.

Emotions are linked to our body and brain and therefore influence our behaviour. It is our behavioural response that determines how long we will be impacted by an emotion.

Our body uses emotional pain to keep us safe.

We increase the amount of positive emotion we experience through practising gratitude, savouring and optimism.

Like a battery, we need both positive and negative emotions to keep us fully charged and working.

A negative emotion is a call to action, whereas a positive emotion is a reward for taking proper action.

Emotional intelligence is when we are managing our emotions rather than being managed by them.

FROM IDEAS TO ACTION

- Choose one or two intentional activities listed in this chapter and commit to doing them for at least a month. During this time, reflect on their impact on your happiness.

- Think back over the last six months and calculate how much of your happiness came from hedonic pursuits (pleasure and enjoyment) and how much from eudaimonic activities (purpose and meaning). Do you think you have the balance right? Are there any adjustments you need to make?

- Practice turning your negative emotions into positive thoughts by deliberately focusing on what is good in a situation. Work hard to prevent negative emotions from impacting you for more than 90 seconds.

- From the list of positive emotions found in this chapter choose one that you'd like to experience more. Use your phone camera to record the times in your life when you experience this emotion. Compile these images into a portfolio. Schedule time in your week to savour the images in your portfolio.

8.
Time and Workload Management

"Working hard and working smart sometimes can be two different things."
- Byron Dorgan

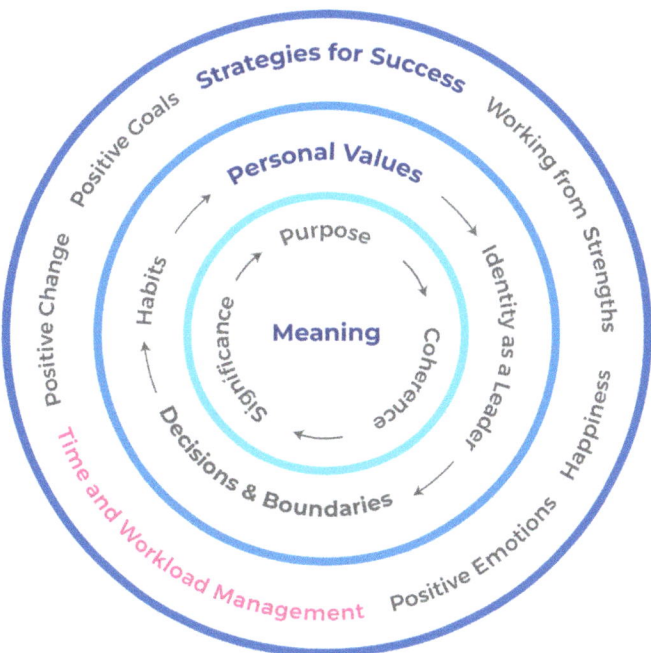

Figure 8.1
Circles of Positive Deviance

Time and workload are inextricably linked. Time is a scarce commodity that we never seem to have enough of, while workload has a habit of expanding to a point that sits just beyond the time we have available. Some workloads are unreasonably excessive, others we allow to become excessive, and still others we are responsible for making excessive. But until we have a good understanding of how we use our time, it is almost impossible to ascertain the reasonableness of our workload.

TIME MANAGEMENT

Time is our most precious commodity. We are all allotted a finite amount, which, if we are lucky enough to live until we are eighty, equates to 4,160 weeks. Even though we never know when our time will be up, we seem to be obsessed with trying to fit more and more into our already overly busy lives. It is so easy to overestimate how much we can achieve in a day and then end up working longer than we should just to keep our heads above water. Proactively managing time enables us to positively deviate away from the overwhelm of having too much to do and not enough time to do it.

Understanding how we spend our time is an important place to start. My favourite way to do this is with a time audit.

A couple of years into my first principalship, my newly appointed deputy principal came to me one Monday morning and asked if she could ask me a rude question. Intrigued, I said of course. She then proceeded to recall a conversation she'd had with her partner the night before about what I did

> all day. She realised that she didn't know, and so the question she'd come to ask me was "What do you do all day?" I remember my reply was "I don't actually know, but I do know that I am really busy." So, I set about to find out.
>
> For that entire week, I recorded what I did about every 15 minutes and then on Friday afternoon I sent the 40-page document to her with the note "This is what I do all day." I also took the time to analyse how I'd spent my time that week and it was such an insight. Until that moment, I hadn't realised that most of my time was taken up with talking to people!

If you've never done an audit of your time, then make this a priority. Commit to doing this over a week, otherwise, you may fall prey to *the Hawthorne Effect*, which is when we change our behaviour because we know it is being observed.[48] We might think we know what our job is, but the reality might be quite different. Prior to me doing my audit, I would have thought that my job was writing the newsletter, meetings, emailing, dealing with misbehaving children, signing accounts, writing reports, and managing property. Yes, I did all of those things. But the thing I did the most, which I probably wouldn't have even listed in my tasks, was lots and lots of talking to people.

Once we know what we are spending our time on each week, we can then begin to figure out if there are ways to make better use of it. This is what I had to do in my principalship. Whilst talking to people is an important part of a leader's role, it is a part that needs to be managed strategically. At the time I did my audit, I wasn't being strategic at all about this. If someone wanted to talk to me, I was available. This is not an approach I'd recommend.

VALUING YOUR TIME

The first lesson in learning how to better manage time is to value our own time. This is important because the amount of value we ascribe to ourselves is directly proportional to the amount of value others will ascribe to us. I've drawn a graph to illustrate this complicated relationship! (Figure 8.2)

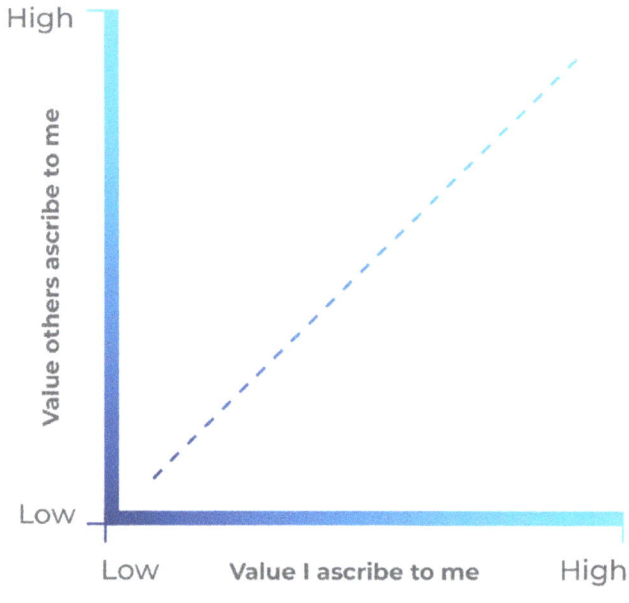

Figure 8.2
Relative Value of Time

In all seriousness though, if we want others to respect our time, we must get our own relationship with time sorted first. It all comes down to the value we ascribe to our time. This is not easy as value represents a relative worth or importance. It is a fine balance. Undervaluing our time risks people taking advantage of us, whereas placing too high a value on our time risks damaging relationships.

Time and Workload Management

So, what is the value we put on our time? A good way to measure this is how we manage that interruption when someone says, "Have you got a minute?" A good test to see if others are valuing our time is to observe whether they pause for us to answer before launching into what they have to say. When someone asks, "Have you got a minute?" and they don't pause, the message they are sending is, "What I have to say is of more value than whatever it is you are doing." When we let people do this unchallenged, we are giving tacit agreement with their view about the relative value of both of our times.

Now, I am not advocating that we shouldn't be available to people. Sometimes, it is the right thing to stop whatever it is we are doing and engage with this person. What I am suggesting though, is that if we don't value our own time and put protective barriers around it, then no one else will value it either. An effective strategy I have used for the "Have you got a minute?" situations is to say, "Not right now, but I really want to hear what it is you have to say, so let's find a time when I can give you my full attention." This response communicates value for the other person, as well as communicating the value I place on my own time.

If it is our boss, or someone more senior to us in an organisation, then the best way to manage this is to suggest an organisation-wide policy around interruptions. We'll look at these types of agreements in more depth in the third book in this series: *Setting Organisations Up for Success*.

One final thing before moving on: lots of leaders pride themselves on their open-door policy. If seeming available is important, then think very carefully about how this is communicated. Does "Open-Door" mean anyone can interrupt at any time, or does it mean you are available to everyone, but at a time that is suitable for both? If it is the latter, it would be wise to think twice before using the phrase "Open-Door" to describe availability.

Another way leaders devalue their time is by letting meetings run over. What message are we communicating when we let people take up more of our time than is necessary? We need strategies ahead of time for this. For those fortunate enough to have an assistant, asking them to interrupt the meeting once the time is up is a helpful strategy. Great assistants will do this irrespective of whether there is actually another engagement. When people see that our time is limited, our value in their eyes will rise, as will their respect, when they can see that we made time for them in the midst of our busyness. For those without an assistant, a useful strategy is to say: "Oh, I see our time is up. I don't want to take up any more of your time than is necessary. Thank you so much for meeting with me." Then get up and move. Note, however, if you don't move straight away, you'll be dealing with a "No, no it is quite all right!" Another strategy is to actually have another meeting to go to immediately afterwards.

TASK-SWITCHING

The second lesson in learning how to better manage our time is to stop task-switching. Many leaders find themselves simultaneously juggling a whole range of tasks, switching rapidly from one thing to another. While this might feel efficient, it is anything but. It is actually wasting time. For years, people have prided themselves on being able to multitask, but scientific studies have shown that humans only have the ability to focus on one task at a time unless it is some physical task that we have learnt to automate (e.g. driving a car while listening to a podcast.) When we try to do more than one thing at a time, we are not multitasking; we are actually task-switching. *Psychology Today*[49] estimates that we lose up to 40% of our productivity when we task-switch and it actually takes more time to complete tasks if we switch between them, rather than do them one at a time. It is also reported that we make more errors when we switch from one task to another.

So how do we move from task-switching to a more focused approach? Stephen Covey's[50] second habit of highly effective people, "begin with the end in mind", can help. Firstly, we need to commit to stopping task-switching and dedicate time to focusing on one task at a time. Once we've decided on this, our next task is to figure out how we are going to do it. Here are some ideas:

Make Email Your Servant, Not Your Master

The simple fact about email is either we control it, or it will control us. Email is probably responsible for more task-switching than anything else. If email notifications cause our focus to switch, then remove the distraction. Try scheduling specific time slots during the day to deal with email. Outside of these times, remove all task-switching temptations, such as leaving the email window open on your browser or notifications on your phone.

Calendar Appointments with Yourself

Schedule focussed time to complete in-depth tasks and treat the appointment as sacrosanct, as if you were meeting with the most important person in your organisation.

Schedule Important Things Early in the Day

Often the important things we need to do are also the hardest, and therefore, the ones we are more likely to be tempted to multi-task over. Generally speaking, there are fewer things to distract us earlier in the day, so there is more chance of remaining focussed.

Work with Your Team

I am constantly amazed that more leadership teams don't work together to carve out 'interruption free' time for each person. I wonder if this is because team members are worried that when they come back from their focused time, there will be even more on their plate to deal with, or if they feel as though they are shirking their responsibilities by allowing others to cover their role.

Treasure Your Noise-Cancelling Headphones

If you work in an open-plan office, then invest in some noise-cancelling headphones or earbuds to remove the temptation to join in the office conversations when you are trying to stay focused. Headphones also communicate the message that you are focused on a task and act as a disincentive to people interrupting you.

MAKING THE BEST USE OF YOUR TIME

It's hard to go past *Eisenhower's Matrix* (made famous by Stephen Covey in his *Seven Habits for Highly Effective People* book) as a model for how to make the best use of our time. It has been my guide throughout my leadership journey, as it not only helps me prioritise my work, but it reduces stress caused by doing things at the last minute.

For those unfamiliar with the matrix, it looks like this (Figure 8.3).

Time and Workload Management

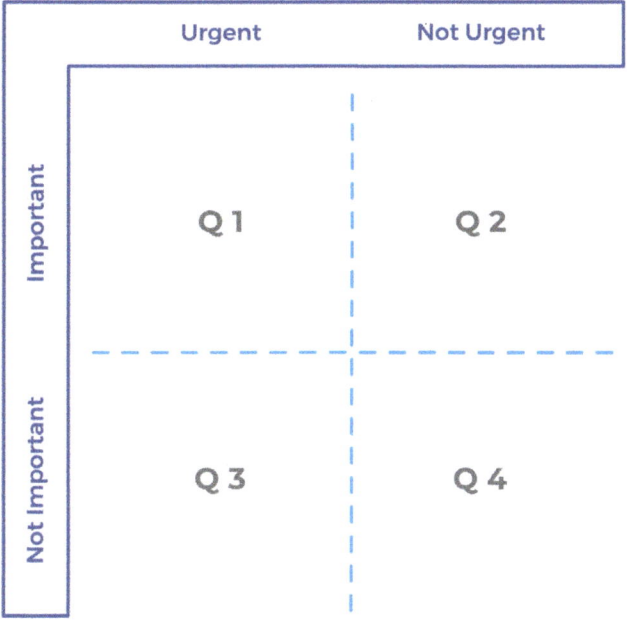

Figure 8.3
Time Management Matrix

Everything we do in life falls into one of these four quadrants. The optimal quadrant is Q2, which is when we are doing important things at a time when they are not urgent. An example of this would be when I write my *Thursday Thinking* blog post on Monday morning. We make the best use of our time when we are working in Q2. We do better work without a looming deadline, and if we can manage to mainly operate in Q2, an unexpected crisis or problem is unlikely to derail us.

Q1 is when we are doing important tasks that are urgent. Some of these we can't avoid, but many we can. For example, leaving writing a funding application to the day before it is due.

Q3 represents the things we do that are urgent but not important. Examples of this are being called to a meeting about something that could have been sorted by email, or helping someone reset a password when we are not our organisation's IT technician. Finding ourselves in Q3 is a great opportunity to reflect on the value we are assigning to our time.

Q4 is the quadrant that will be either a trivial or a time-wasting activity; for example, mindlessly scrolling through social media. It may also be a pleasant activity that is neither urgent nor important but is fun. Whilst there are times when we will end up in Q1, Q3 or Q4, spending as much time as possible in Q2 makes the very best use of the time we have available.

WORKLOAD MANAGEMENT

Once we understand how we are spending our time, the value we place on it, the inefficiency of task-switching and the benefit of being in Q2, we are now ready to look objectively at workload management.

Tasks Need to be Meaningful

The first thing to consider is how much of our time is spent on tasks that are meaningful work. Not everything we do will be directly contributing to fulfilling our purpose, but if we are in the right job, there should be a link between the things we spend most of our time on and the meaning we create through our work. Sometimes, we are so busy getting on with our tasks, that we overlook the connection between what we are doing and our purpose. This can happen to me when I have been away from home a lot. I sometimes catch myself mentally going through a list of things I need to do before I get to go home, rather than thinking about how the tasks ahead of me contribute to the purpose for my life.

Tasks Need to be High-Value

The second thing to consider is whether the things we spend our time on are the things that deliver the best value to our organisation. A way I used to figure this out was to work out my hourly rate. I then thought about the tasks I did in the course of a day, and then considered whether I'd pay someone else my hourly rate to do that job. When the answer was no, then I knew that task was not part of my workload. This didn't necessarily lead to me not doing the task, but this hourly rate calculation gave me a useful perspective on how I was using my time.

Another way of looking at the value you are delivering your organisation is that if you are in a senior role, there will be very few people getting that level of remuneration. If you spend your time doing tasks that are not reflective of your hourly rate, then your organisation is not getting the full benefit of the money they are investing in you. It comes down to being very strategic about how you use your time.

Imagine you are a senior leader of a mid-sized organisation. Each morning, when you arrive at work, you go into the kitchen and make a plunger of coffee. As people arrive for the day, you pour them a coffee. Now applying the rule above, is making coffee something a senior leader should be doing? Would you be willing to pay your local barista the same hourly rate for making your coffee as a senior leader gets? Obviously not.

However, if the reason you, as a senior leader, are making the coffee is that it is an effective way to check in with each member of your team at the start of the day, then this activity is worth your hourly rate.

Tasks Need to be Manageable

Identifying what is an acceptable and manageable workload is tricky. I have been in many senior roles, and I know that one of the hallmarks of being a senior leader is that you are generally willing to go above and beyond to get things done. It's this attitude that often gets people promoted. From time to time, it is important that leaders roll up their sleeves and go the extra mile. But this becomes a problem if leaders end up constantly doing the jobs no one else is willing to do. Manageability of tasks and our ability to cope with changes varies, sometimes hourly, depending on situations and our individual capability at any given time. When things are going well, an extra task is easy to manage, but when we are really under pressure, that one small extra job could be the final straw. Sometimes we need to remember to:

"Go easy on yourself.
Whatever you do today, let it be enough."
- Unknown

However, if we know that we are managing our time well, but are ending up having to work excessive hours every week to keep up, then it might be that we are dealing with an unreasonable workload. Alternatively, we might have forgotten Parkinson's Law, which states:

"Work expands so as to fill
the time available for its completion."
– C. Northcote Parkinson

A good way to check in around Parkinson's Law is to listen to our response whenever anyone asks us how work is going. If our typical reply is about how busy we are, we need to stop and check that we haven't formed a belief that being busy is linked to importance. This is the type of thinking that expands roles to be bigger than they need to be. It also means we are accepting a work situation that we're not happy with. Don't. Do something to fix it.

A good strategy to address excessive workload is to go back to your job description and record the average time spent each week against each part of your job. You might use the time audit suggested at the start of this chapter to help you. If this adds up to more hours than you are employed for, or the hours you are willing to give a job, then it is time to figure out how to re-prioritise your work so that it fits into the time allocated. You could also use this exercise to highlight the things you regularly do that are not part of your job description.

Tasks Need to be Traded

Role expansion is another contributor to excessive workloads. This happens when we have an additive approach rather than a replacement approach to change. Role expansion is often driven from a place of wanting to continually grow and improve. But, we need to train ourselves to name what it is we are going to stop doing, in order to create the space necessary for this new thing we want to do. This is important at both the organisational and individual levels. Whenever we say yes to something, we are also saying no to something else. Make sure this is an active choice, not an accidental consequence. It is much easier to stop workloads from becoming excessive than to pick up the pieces when everything has become all too much.

CHAPTER SUMMARY
Time and Workload Management

Time is a scarce commodity that we never seem to have enough of, while workloads have a habit of expanding to just beyond the time we have available.

The amount of value we ascribe to our time is directly proportional to the amount of value others will ascribe to it.

Task-switching isn't being efficient with time, it is wasting time. We lose 40% of our productivity when we task-switch.

It is better to do important jobs when they are not urgent.

There should be a link between the things we spend the most time on and our purpose.

Thinking of our tasks in terms of an hourly rate is a good way to measure if what we are doing is delivering value to our organisation.

Role expansion contributes to work overload. Whenever we say yes to something, we are saying no to something else.

FROM IDEAS TO ACTION

- Do a time audit over five days. Try to pause once an hour and record what it is you have been doing. At the end of your audit, analyse into categories, how you spent your time. (i.e. relationship building, report writing, responding to emails, one-on-ones etc.) Calculate how much time you spent in each category. Identify any categories where you are over-spending or underspending your time.

- Do a second analysis of your time audit using the Time Management Matrix (Figure 8.3). How much time are you spending in each quadrant? Are there any changes you might make to increase your time in Q2 (Important but Not Urgent)?

- Challenge yourself to find one hour a day when you don't task-switch. Over time, see if you can increase your focused time.

- Compare your time audit with your job description. Is there anything you are spending time on that is outside your job description? Is there anything in your job description that you are not spending time doing?

- Take a moment to reflect on how your job has changed over the past few years. Can you identify additions or subtractions to your workload? Does your job description need to be updated?

9.
Positive Change and Positive Goals

"Between stimulus and response there is a space. In that space is our power to choose our response. In our response lies our growth and our freedom."
- Viktor E. Frankl

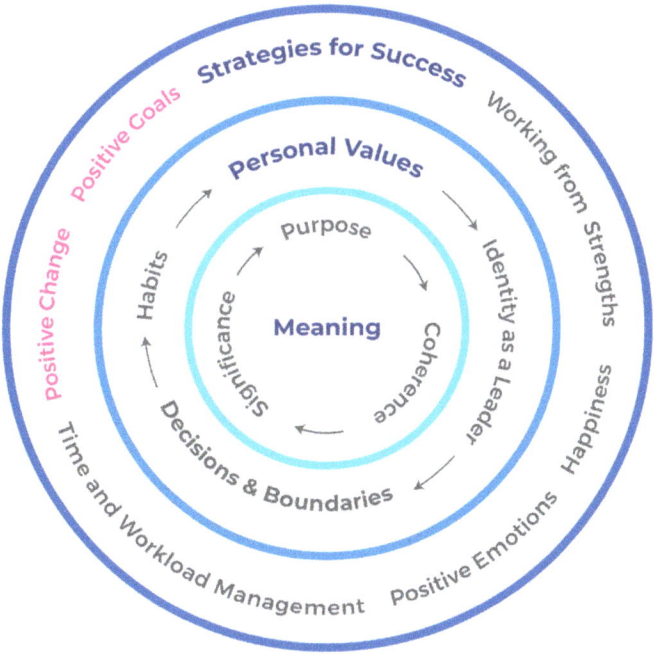

Figure 9.1
Circles of Positive Deviance

We now come to the final two Strategies for Success: *positive change* and *positive goals*. Like happiness and positive emotions, positive change and positive goals also have a symbiotic relationship. We set goals when we want to change, and we change because of the goals we have set. While they are two different strategies for success, they are best thought of in relation to each other.

We are in a constant state of change. Change can either be a positive experience or a negative one. Just like emotions, we can't always control the change we experience, but we can control how we respond to it. At times we will be causing the change. At other times change will be driven by forces or circumstances beyond our control. Generally speaking, negative change is the result of us standing back and allowing unwelcome change to happen to us. On the other hand, positive change is the change, whether it is welcome or unwelcome, that we lead.

Change is inevitable and constant, but even in the midst of unwelcome change, there are still choices to be made, the biggest one being whether we will lead the change or let the change happen to us. Positive change generally starts with us setting ourselves a goal.

For example, in Chapter Five, I talked about the goal my husband and I set to be better, not bitter, as we came to terms with and navigated my younger brother's death. The change we are driving will always have a more positive outcome than change that is done to us. Change can result in a more meaningful life or see us living even more aligned with our values; change can lead to habits that enable us to thrive and not just survive as a leader.

The best way to ensure positive change is through positive goal- setting. In this chapter, we explore not only the best time and way to change but we will also look at how to set goals that have the greatest chance of being achieved.

POSITIVE CHANGE

> *"If we don't change, we don't grow.*
> *If we don't grow, we aren't really living."*
> *- Gail Sheehy*

Whether we like it or not, change is a constant in all of our lives. Sometimes change takes us closer to the life we aspire to have, and at other times, it feels like it is taking us further away. Change is constant and if we resist it, we end up going backwards. It is not possible to stay still, because everything around us is moving and changing.

Change Happening to Us

The way to make our change experiences as positive as possible is to lead them. We need to be the ones writing the story of our lives, not sitting back and letting others write it for us. Being the one leading a change can make a change positive, even in negative situations.

I had a colleague who found themselves in an awful position at work. They were being targeted by two bullies whose behaviour the rest of the company preferred to ignore rather than address. In the end, they sought professional help and were advised to hire a lawyer, which they did. With the lawyer's help, they were able to manage their exit from this toxic work

environment. This person talked about how different they felt before and after engaging the lawyer. Before the lawyer, they felt unable to effect change and were just letting whatever happened, happen. Once they got a lawyer, they felt empowered because they were able to start leading the change process. This made it a positive overall experience for them.

An example of proactive change is when older people sell their family home and downsize before everything gets too much for them. This means that they manage the change, rather than having the change managed for them by younger members of their family.

> *"Change before you have to."*
> *- Jack Welch*

Managing change before you have to change does not just apply to older people moving out of their family homes. It also applies to parenting. Our children are designed to transition into young adults. If at this point parents don't change their strategies, then their young adult will certainly "help" them do it. When it comes to managing change in our jobs, we never want to be that person that everyone breathes a sigh of relief over when we finally hand in our resignation. Some people stay in jobs because the thought of change is too scary. Yet, so often these very same people, when they eventually do leave or are "helped" to leave, find a job that is much more fulfilling and meaningful.

Change We Initiate

So far, we have looked at how to positively manage the change that is happening to you. Now it is time to explore the positive change that we initiate and lead. This is the positive change that leads to professional growth and success. The main thing we have to learn as a leader is how early we should be starting these change processes. I find the Sigmoid Curve[51] a useful model when thinking about this (Figure 9.2).

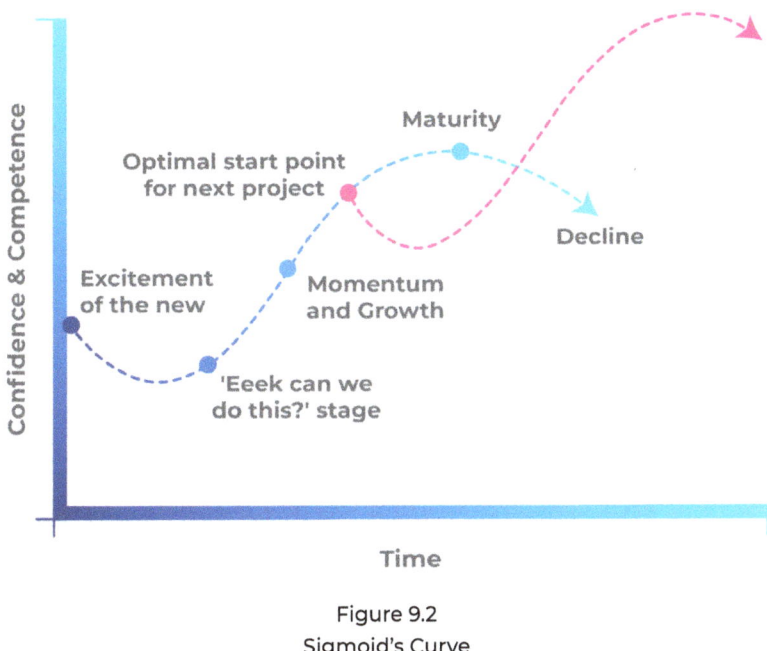

Figure 9.2
Sigmoid's Curve

The first line shows the trajectory of something new. This might be a job, a project or an initiative. We start out feeling confident, but as the reality of what is in front of us begins to bite, our confidence takes a dip. I remember this happening to me when I accepted my first senior leadership role. I was really confident at the interview and I must have come across as competent, because they offered me the role, which I accepted. However, the next morning my confidence and competence took a dive as I started to think about what I'd agreed to take on.

If we understand this confidence and competence dip, we can reassure ourselves that this is something everyone experiences and it doesn't mean we are about to fail. The worst thing we can do when we are in the implementation dip is to retrench back to what we have always done. Instead, we need to hold our course and, in time, the curve will begin to rise.

As our confidence and competence begin to increase, we will gather momentum and start to experience growth. It is at this point that we need to embark on our next job, project or initiative. We need to have something new in place before what we are currently doing matures, and then predictably begins to decline. Positive change happens when we have something new gathering momentum and growing at the same time as something else is declining.

Writing this book is an example of me starting something new while I am still on the momentum and growth curve. I have not yet reached maturity with my current work, but I also know that if I keep doing what I am currently doing, the time will come when the abundance I am enjoying now will start to dry up. It is also much easier to promote a book and Masterclass to an audience I am fully engaged with.

This is not the first time I have pivoted in my career during a period of momentum and growth. As I mentioned earlier in this book, in 2013 I resigned from my principalship of a school that was, at the time, seen as a flagship for digital practice in New Zealand. The circumstances for my leaving come from an unexpected job offer to a senior role in a company established by our government to roll out fibre connectivity to every school in New Zealand. Taking that job gave me the opportunity to add business and senior government experience to my educational leadership expertise and now underpins the success of my current work.

Even though we might understand how applying the Sigmoid

Curve to our lives produces positive change, it still takes grit and determination. This is because we need to start our next challenge at the very time we are experiencing the growth and momentum that comes from feeling confident and competent in the work that we do. The temptation to settle is huge, but if we do, we can end up paying a considerable price.

I learnt an important lesson about the dangers of settling from one of our native birds, the kawau:

There is a gorgeous lagoon walk not far from where we live. One of the things I love about the walk is that it passes nesting sites for kawau (shags). One time we did the walk we came across a large tree that was absolutely full of nesting kawau. A year later we did the walk again. This time the tree which had previously been overloaded with nesting kawau, had only one or two nests left. We could also see that many of the tree's branches had been chopped down.

I was feeling sad that the kawau had lost their nesting site, until one of the friends we were walking with explained that the kawau droppings actually leach into the soil around the tree, eventually killing it. This put quite a different spin on the situation.

On the other side of the lagoon, we came to the next tree the kawau had taken over. Already the tree was starting to suffer from having the kawau settling in its branches. The danger of kawau settling, content in the abundance of their current nesting site, is that the tree has already begun its decline.

If you feel like you have settled, then don't panic. All is not lost. It is never too late to start something new. As I look back over my life, there have been several times when I settled, staying too long in a job. The challenge with starting something new after we've reached maturity in our current situation is that we don't have the momentum and growth from our current role to buoy us along.

We always need to remember that positive change occurs in two spaces. Firstly, when we step in and lead the change that is happening to us, and secondly, stepping up to lead change that results in continuous growth.

> *"Change will not come if we wait for some other person or some other time. We are the ones we've been waiting for. We are the change we seek."*
> *- Barack Obama*

POSITIVE GOALS

The best way to manage change is to set goals that reflect the change we seek. Goals might be formally constructed, or they might be a response to an unexpected situation we encounter. For example, when we decided that my brother's illness was going to make us better people, not bitter, we didn't sit down in a formal goal-setting situation or write the goal on a post-it note for our fridge. The goal was a determination we said out loud and continued to say out loud every time the journey got tough. At other times, I have deliberately set goals that I have reminded myself of every day until I achieved them.

But not all goals are created equal. Some goals have a much higher chance of being achieved than others. This is perhaps best illustrated by Christian Ehrlich's[52] Goal-Striving Framework (Figure 9.3).

Figure 9.3
Goal-Striving Framework

According to Ehrlich, the goals we are most likely to reach are the ones sitting in the left-hand quadrants. These are the goals that are pursued because they help others or are pursued out of pleasure. Helping others and pleasure are strongly correlated to happiness and positive emotions. These are positive goals. The quadrants on the right-hand side are the goals less likely to be achieved. They are negative goals that have unpleasant consequences attached to them. We are much more likely to reach goals that are pleasurable or help others.

Setting goals is at the very heart of positive deviance. Deviating from our current way of being starts with the setting of goals that lead to positive change. As a leader, we need to keep working on ourselves. The problem is that when the pressure comes on, it is easy to put our head down and just plough through whatever is in front of us. Sometimes leading feels like a game of 'Whack-a-Mole'. Just as we manage to whack one mole into its place, another is popping up, begging for our attention. But in our one lifetime, there is only so much we can achieve, and no matter how hard we work, there will always be more to do. So, it is vitally important that the goals we set for ourselves are ones that will help us thrive and take us closer to becoming the leader we aspire to be.

Positive goals are the ones that reflect our purpose, bringing meaning to our lives. They align with the identity we hold as a leader and will often be the bridge between the leader we are today and the one we are aspiring to become. Positive goals use our strengths and result in us experiencing positive emotions.

For years I have struggled with the concept of SMART goals. For the uninitiated, the acronym stands for Specific, Measurable, Achievable, Realistic, and Time-Bound. No one knows who first came up with the concept, but it is a widely adopted approach, probably because they are tangible and easy to measure. I think that what is at the heart of my dislike for the SMART goal approach is that they never seem to result in meaningful change. I am not alone in this thinking. Leadership IQ[53] studied more than 16,000 people and found that SMART goals actually lead to lower performance and people being far less likely to love their jobs. Another challenge with SMART is goals have to be achievable and realistic. If goals are attached to a salary payment or professional registration, we are hardly likely to choose something we won't achieve. This is problematic because the optimal conditions to achieve, as described by Mihaly Csikszentmihalyi's[54] theory of flow occur,

Positive Change and Positive Goals

"when a person's body or mind is stretched to its limits in a voluntary effort to accomplish something difficult and worthwhile. Optimal experience is thus something we make happen."

So how do you go about setting positive goals in a way that increases your likelihood of achieving them? I'd recommend setting yourself up with a canvas that looks a bit like the one in Figure 9.4.

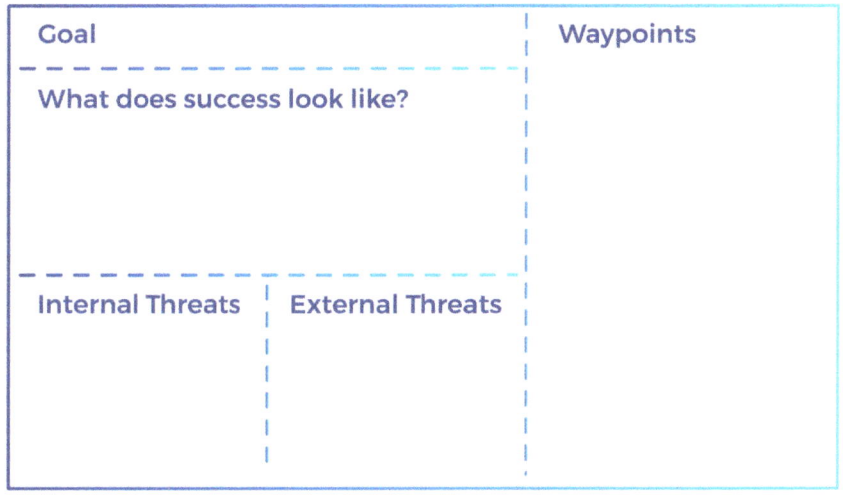

Figure 9.4
Goal-Setting Canvas

1. Choose a goal that sits on the left-hand side of Ehrlich's[55] framework. It will be a positive goal in that it will either help others or bring pleasure. Think about what would make your life more meaningful or take you closer to the leader you aspire to be.

2. Next, articulate what success will look like. This helps to clarify exactly what is to be achieved. This description might include reference to your purpose, values and/or the leader you aspire to be.

3. Identifying the threats that might hinder you from reaching your goal is important. There are two types of threats that need to be identified. Internal threats are those you can control and external threats are those you can't. Recording threats makes them real, and will set you on the path of thinking about how you might ameliorate them.

4. Finally, identify your Waypoints.

Waypoints replace an action plan. The problem with action plans is that they are generally out-of-date before we get very far down the list of action points. Waypoints are a much better strategy.

> *"Every journey needs some kind of map of waypoints,*
> *and these are important signifiers*
> *that we are on track to reach a goal."*
> *- Wayfinding Leadership*

The waypoints described here are like the markers that yachts sail around during the course of a race. Skippers don't leave the harbour with a step-by-step set of instructions as to how they are going to sail between the markers. What they do have is knowledge about how their boat sails, the skills of the crew, the weather, and the sea conditions. They use all of this information, as well as observing what is and isn't working for the other boats, to set and keep adjusting their course as they sail towards the next waypoint. This is a great metaphor for navigating goals.

List in the Waypoint box the key things you will need to achieve in order to reach your goal. These will help you stay on track whilst giving you the ability to change course in response to the conditions.

Positive deviance begins with positive goals leading to positive change. This is an important key to thriving as a leader.

CHAPTER SUMMARY
Positive Change and Positive Goals

Change can either be a positive experience or a negative one. We can't always control change, but we can control our response to it. We can either lead the change or let the change lead us. The change we are leading will always be more positive than the change that is done to us.

Positive change that leads to professional growth and success is generally the change we have initiated. The Sigmoid Curve is a useful model to explain sustaining momentum around change. We need to springboard our next challenge off the momentum of our current one.

The goals we are more likely to reach are the ones that are pursued out of pleasure or to help others. Positively deviating from our current way of being starts with the setting of goals that lead to positive change.

Research shows that SMART goals actually lead to lower performance and people being far less likely to love their jobs. Using Waypoints helps us stay on track while giving us the ability to change course in response to the conditions.

FROM IDEAS TO ACTION

- Make a list of all the significant changes you've had in your life. Think about each change and note whether it was something you initiated or something that happened to you. What are some strategies you use to help you manage change? What might stop you from making necessary changes?

- As you near the end of this book, think about any actions you might want to take as a result of what you have learnt. How might you turn these into positive goals?

- Set yourself up a canvas, similar to Figure 9.4, and create a plan to help you achieve your goals. Have a go at setting some waypoints and see if these serve you better than bullet points on an action plan.

10.
Packed and Ready

"Before anything else, preparation is the key to success."
- Alexander Graham Bell

On my way to the airport, I often have panicked thoughts about whether I remembered to pack everything I needed for my trip. Invariably I have, and even though I know this, it is not unusual to find myself rifling through my suitcase just to check. In a sense, this final chapter is our chance to rifle through this first packing cell in the Leader's Suitcase to check we have the materials we need packed and ready for our journey.

Early on in the book, we talked about this packing cell containing the things that we mainly use by ourselves. It is the very personal things that we use to ensure that as leaders, we thrive and not just survive. The motivation behind this first packing cell was to positively deviate either from our current actions or from the way others around us are responding to our current circumstances. Being a positive deviant is not about being better than others. It's about being a better version of ourselves, something that is always highly desirable. It is about positively deviating from the norm of our current existence. Throughout the book, we have used the three Circles of Positive Deviance (Figure 10.1) to give us an overview of the things needed to deviate positively from the norm.

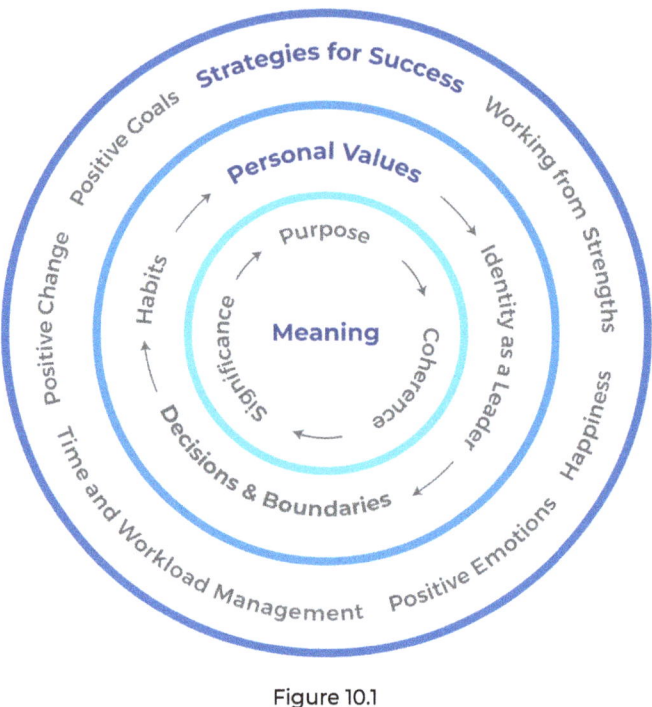

Figure 10.1
Circles of Positive Deviance

INNER CIRCLE

The most essential piece of material to have in this first packing cell is meaning. Meaning, with its three interrelated components of purpose, coherence and significance, is the "why" for our work as a leader. A meaningful life starts with purpose - the reason we were put on this earth. Without a clear purpose, it is very difficult to see the coherence of our lives and to know for certain that what we are doing matters. When the going gets tough, and from time to time it will, reminding ourselves of our purpose will produce the much-needed positive deviance spark. In addition, understanding our purpose helps us make sense of our journey and gives us confidence that our life has significance.

We know meaning is present in our packing cell when we can answer the following questions:

1. As a leader my purpose is to ...
2. In my life right now this looks like ...
3. What I do matters because ...

SECOND CIRCLE

The second Circle of Positive Deviance is about how we lead. It starts with a conscious understanding of the values which are most important to us. We use these personal values to craft the identity of the leader we aspire to be. A good way to do this is to write declarations that reflect how we want others to experience our leadership. We know this is in our packing cell when we can name our top six personal values and have declarations that reinforce our leadership identity.

Personal Values	Declarations
1.	
2.	
3.	
4.	
5.	
6.	

Figure 10.2
Values and Declaration Mapping Tool

Having established the identity of the leader we aspire to be, we are then set up to make decisions and keep boundaries that are aligned to our values. We know this resource is safely stowed in our packing case when, over time, these become the habits that reinforce our personal values.

THIRD CIRCLE

The third Circle of Positive Deviance contains strategies we can employ to positively deviate from our current circumstances. Some of these strategies we will be using regularly, while others would benefit from an increased focus. While the strategies can be focussed on in any order, following them clockwise around the circle will give the greatest benefit.

Here are some ways to know if our strategies for success are packed and ready in this first packing cell of the Leader's Suitcase. These questions and activities are provided to help you identify the things you already have in your packing cell and the resources you are missing. The activities are intended to help you identify where you might focus next.

Working from Strengths

Completing the following statements will test that the "working from strengths" resource is packed and ready:

1. The strengths which serve me best are:
   -
   -
   -
   -
   -

2. I am working from my strengths when ...
3. A strength I am in danger of over-using is ...
4. To ensure I don't, I will ...
5. Strengths I need to use carefully in order to maintain my energy levels are:
   -
   -
   -

6. To support my weakness of ... I will ...

Happiness and Positive Emotions

Completing the following tables will test if the happiness and positive emotions material is packed and ready:

In the last week I have been intentional in taking the following actions to increase my happiness:

Intentional Action	Yes/No	Activity
Gratitude		
Helping Others		
Acts of Kindness		
Nurturing Relationships		
Savouring Life's Pleasures		

Figure 10.3
Intentional Activity Matrix

In the last week I am aware of experiencing the following emotions:

Positive Emotion	Narrative
Negative Emotion	**Narrative**

Figure 10.4
Emotion Matrix

Time and Workload Management

Completing the following statements will test if time and workload management resources are packed and ready:

I spend the majority of my time ...
In the last two weeks I spent the following percentage of time in each matrix:

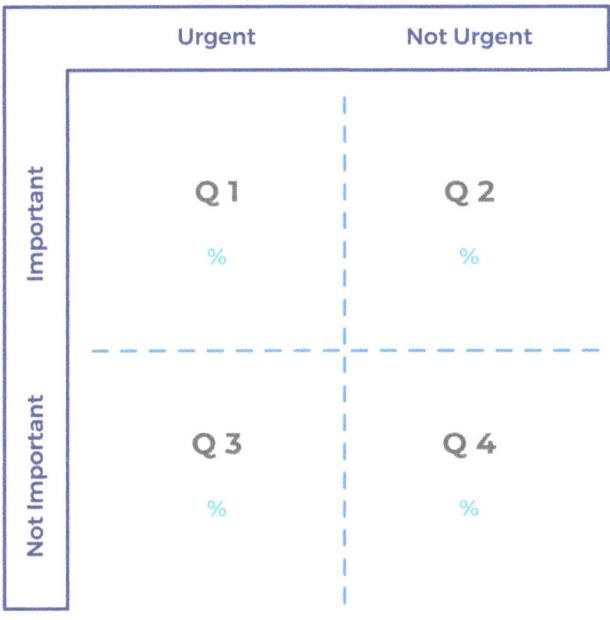

Figure 10.5
Time Management Percentage Grid

I end up in Q1 when ...
I spend time in Q3 when ...
In the last 12 months, the following changes have been made to my role ...

Positive Change and Positive Goals

A positive goal, which helps others or is something I would enjoy, that I have set for myself is …

The waypoints for this goal are …

READY SET GO

If you've reached this stage of the book and you can see that your packing cell is incomplete, then don't fret. We are going to spend a lifetime gathering and adapting the material we need for our leadership journey. Some things you will have already stowed ahead of reading this book, while some may have been packed along the way. Still other material will be things you haven't gotten to yet, and that is okay. Leadership is a journey.

Whenever I am preparing to go away, I find it helpful to prioritise specific time to pack. This ensures that when it is time to leave, I feel calm and confident in the knowledge that I have packed wisely for the journey ahead. The same is true for our leadership journey. Prioritising time to check, and if necessary, replenish the contents of our Leader's Suitcase is the best way to ensure our leadership success.

Along with writing this book, I have designed a Masterclass, which will help you prioritise packing the things into your Leader's Suitcase that will set you up for success. Delivered online, these Masterclasses are a collaborative adventure, learning about and then applying the Circles of Positive Deviance to our lives. The goal of the Masterclass is to transform leaders into positive deviants.

This QR code will take you to my website where you can find out more.

Packing Cell Two: Setting Others Up for Success

In the Leader's Suitcase there are three packing cells.

1. Setting Yourself Up for Success
2. Setting Others Up for Success
3. Setting Organisations Up for Success.

If you've gotten to this part of the book about the first packing cell, then I'm going to assume that you are well on your way to setting yourself up for success. That means it's now time to start thinking about what comes next as a leader. Leaders have many functions, but the one I think is the most important is in *Packing Cell Two: Setting Others Up for Success*.

In *Packing Cell Two*, we explore how to lead with empathy and in a way that supports and challenges everyone to be the best version of themselves. Authentic relationships, built on trust, sit at the heart of this work. The people we lead need to know they can trust us, and we, in turn, need to be able to trust them. The people we lead also need to be able to trust each other. Growing high-functioning teams, that work together so that everyone meets their accountabilities, is some of the most important work a leader does.

Setting others up for success is also about knowing what we do when we are at our best. That way, we lead from a place of strength, using approaches that others gain the most benefit from. Too often we focus on trying to "fix" ourselves and others. This packing cell is about strengthening the things we do well and supporting others to do the same.

Packing Cell Three: Setting Organisations Up for Success

Where *Packing Cells One* and *Two* are about setting ourselves and others up for success, *Packing Cell Three* explores setting entire organisations up for success. At the heart of every successful organisation is a compelling vision that gives purpose and meaning to the work. Senior leaders are responsible for the strategy that enacts the vision and for the setting of priorities giving the organisation momentum.

At the heart of all strategy is organisational change. This book explores the use of Design Thinking as a methodology to underpin change. Design Thinking brings a disciplined approach to human-centred change. This means people in our organisation are an integral part of the change journey, ensuring change is done with people, rather than to people. Designing, prototyping and testing strategies ahead of full-scale implementation is an important part of this work.

Team leaders operationalise the strategy. They work with their teams to align the day-to-day work with the organisation's priorities. Leaders across the organisation oversee systems and processes ensuring people are empowered to act within their area of expertise.

While senior leaders hold the ultimate responsibility for organisational success, this packing cell equips all leaders to set their part of the organisation up for success.

References

1. Wishik, SM., Van der Vynckt, S. (1976). The use of nutritional "positive deviants" to identify approaches for modification of dietary practices. Am J Public Health. 66(1):38-42. https://doi.org/10.2105/AJPH.66.1.38.

2. Positive Deviance Collaborative. *Positive deviance*. Retrieved from http://positivedeviance.org/ January 2023.

3. Gaba, S. (2020). *Understanding Fight, Flight, Freeze and the Fawn Response*. Retrieved January 2023 from https://www.psychologytoday.com/nz/blog/addiction-and-recovery/202008/understanding-fight-flight-freeze-and-the-fawn-response.

4. Cuddy, A. (2012). *Your body language may shape who you are*. https://www.ted.com/talks/amy_cuddy_your_body_language_may_shape_who_you_are/comments.

5. Positive Psychology White Paper. Retrieved January 2023 from https://langleygroup.com.au/whitepaper-the-science-and-practice-of-positive-psychology/

6. Seligman, M. (1999). Summit 1999 Speech by Martin Seligman. Retrieved March 2023 from https://ppc.sas.upenn.edu/opportunities/conference-archives.

7. Seligman, M. E. (2011). *Flourish: A New Understanding of Happiness and Well-Being and How to Achieve Them*. Boston, MA: Nicholas Brealey Pub.

8. Sinek, S. (2009). The Golden Circle. Retrieved January 2023 from Simon Sinek - The Golden Circle - TedTalks 2009.

9. Steger, M. F. (2012). Experiencing meaning in life—Optimal functioning at the nexus of well-being, psychopathology, and spirituality. In P. T. P. Wong (Ed.), *The human quest for meaning:*

Theories, research, and applications. 2nd edition (pp. 165–184). Routledge.

10. Wong, P. T. P. (2010). Meaning therapy: An integrative and positive existential psychotherapy. *Journal of Contemporary Psychotherapy, 40(2)*, 85–93. https://doi.org/10.1007/s10879-009-9132-6.

11. Positive Psychology White Paper. Retrieved January 2023 from https://langleygroup.com.au/whitepaper-the-science-and-practice-of-positive-psychology/

12. Wong, P. T. P. (2010). Meaning therapy: An integrative and positive existential psychotherapy. *Journal of Contemporary Psychotherapy, 40(2)*, 85–93. https://doi.org/10.1007/s10879-009-9132-6.

13. Martela, F. & Steger, M. F. (2016). The three meanings of meaning in life: Coherence, purpose and significance as the three facets of meaning. *Journal of Positive Psychology, 11(5)*, 531–545. https://doi.org/10.1080/17439760.2015.1137623.

14. Viktor, F. (2006). *Man's Search for Meaning*. London, United Kingdom: Beacon Press.

15. Collins, J. & Lazier, B. (2020). *Beyond Entrepreneurship 2.0* (p. 158). Portfolio/Penguin. Kindle Edition.

16. Csikszentmihalyi, M. (1990). *Flow: The Psychology of Optimal Experience*. New York, NY: Harper and Row.

17. Rogers, B. A., Chicas, H., Kelly, J. M., Kubin, E., Christian, M. S., Kachanoff, F. J., Berger, J., Puryear, C., McAdams, D. P., & Gray, K. (2023). Seeing your life story as a Hero's Journey increases meaning in life. *Journal of Personality and Social Psychology. Advanced online publication.* https://doi.org/10.1037/pspa0000341.

18. Campbell, J. (1949). *The Hero with a Thousand Faces*. 1st edition. USA: Bollingen Foundation/Pantheon Books.

19. Steger, M. F. (2012). Experiencing meaning in life: Optimal functioning at the nexus of well-being, psychopathology, and spirituality. In P. T. P. Wong (Ed.), *The human quest for meaning: Theories, research, and applications* (pp. 165–184). Routledge/Taylor & Francis Group.

20. Values Profile. Retrieved March 2023 from https://www.psychologytoday.com/nz/tests/personality/values-profile.

21. Personal Values Assessment - retrieved March 2023 from https://personalvalu.es/

22. Moore, G. (2014). *Crossing the Chasm*. 3rd Edition. New York: HarperCollins.

23. Cloud, H. & Townsend, J. (1992). *Boundaries*. Michigan: Zondervan.

24. Clear, J. (2018). *Atomic Habits* (p. 1). New York, NY: Random House. Kindle Edition.

25. Gaines, J. (2021). Retrieved March 2023 from https://positivepsychology.com/how-habits-are-formed/

26. Clear, J. (2018). *Atomic Habits* (p. 1). New York, NY: Random House. Kindle Edition.

27. Baumeister, R.F., Bratslavsky, E., Finkenauer, C. & Vohs, K.D. (2001). Bad is stronger than good. *Review of General Psychology*, 5: 323–70.

28. Collins, J. & Lazier, B. (2020). *Beyond Entrepreneurship 2.0* (p. 158). Portfolio/Penguin. Kindle Edition.

29. Govindji, R., & Linley, P. A. (2007). Strengths use, self-concordance and well-being: Implications for strengths coaching and coaching psychologists. *International Coaching Psychology Review, 2(2)*, 143–153.

30. Proctor, C., Linley, P. A., & Maltby, J. (2009). Youth life satisfaction measures: A review. *The Journal of Positive Psychology, 4(2)*, 128–144. https://doi.org/10.1080/17439760802650816

31. Wood, A. M., Linley, P. A., Maltby, J., Kashdan, T. B., & Hurling, R. (2011). Using personal and psychological strengths leads to increases in well-being over time: A longitudinal study and the development of the strengths use questionnaire. *Personality and Individual Differences, 50(1),* 15–19. https://doi.org/10.1016/j.paid.2010.08.004

32. Linley, P.A. (2008). *Average to A+: Realising strengths in yourself and others.* Coventry, UK: CAPP Press.

33. Cameron, K.S., Dutton, J.E., & Quinn, R.E. (2009). Foundations of positive organizational scholarship.

34. Values in Action Institute on Character. *A Simple model for working with strengths.* Retrieved April 2023 from https://www.viacharacter.org/topics/articles/a-simple-model-for-working-with-strengths

35. Values in Action Online Assessment - https://www.viacharacter.org/

36. Linley, P.A. (2010). The business case for a strengths-based organisation. Fact–sheet. *Centre for Applied Positive Psychology.*

37. Roche & Heffron (2013). 'The assessment needs to go hand-in-hand with the debriefing': The importance of a structured coaching debriefing in understanding and applying a positive psychology strengths assessment. *International Coaching Psychology Review, 8(1), 20-34.*

38. Linley, P.A. (2008). *Average to A+: Realising strengths in yourself and others.* Coventry, UK: CAPP Press.

39. Puff, R. (2017) *Your Set Point for Happiness.* Retrieved May 2023 from: https://www.psychologytoday.com/nz/blog/meditation-for-modern-life/201709/your-set-point-for-happiness

40. Lyubomirsky, S (2017). *Is it possible to be happier and, if yes how?* Retrieved March 2022 from https://www.youtube.com/watch?v=ohsAWiCC0YE

References

41. Lyubomirsky, S. (2017). *Is it possible to be happier and, if yes how?* Retrieved March 2022 from https://www.youtube.com/watch?v=ohsAWiCC0YE

42. Lyubomirsky, S., King, L., & Diener, E. (2005). The Benefits of Frequent Positive Affect: Does Happiness Lead to Success? *Psychological Bulletin*, 131(6), 803-855.

43. Lyubomirsky, S., King, L., & Diener, E. (2005). The Benefits of Frequent Positive Affect: Does Happiness Lead to Success? Psychological Bulletin, 131(6), 803-855.

44. Jill Bolte Taylor https://www.drjilltaylor.com/about-dr-jill/

45. Taylor, J. B. (2006). *My Stroke of Insight: A Brain Scientist's Personal Journey*. New York: Viking.

46. Fredrickson, B. L. (2009). *Positivity: Top-notch research reveals the upward spiral that will change your life*. New York, NY: Crown Publishing Group.

47. Fredrickson, B. L. (2001). The role of positive emotions in positive psychology: The broaden-and-build theory of positive emotions. *American Psychologist*, 56(3), 218-226.

48. *Hawthorne effect - this is where you modify your behaviour because you know you are being observed.*

49. Weinschenk, S. (2012). *The True Cost of Multi-Tasking*. Retrieved March 2023 from https://www.psychologytoday.com/us/blog/brain-wise/201209/the-true-cost-of-multi-tasking

50. Covey, S.R. (1989). *Seven Habits of Highly Effective People: Restoring the Character Ethic*. New York: Simon and Shuster.

51. Hipkins, R. & Cowie, B. (2016). The Sigmoid Curve as a metaphor for growth and change. Teachers and Curriculum, 16 (2), 3-9.

52. Ehrlich, C (2019). *The goal-striving framework: Further evidence for its predictive power for subjective well-being on a sub-dimensional level and on an individual goal-striving*

reasons level as well as evidence for its theoretical difference to self-concordance*. Oxford, United Kingdom: Oxford Brooks University. Retrieved March 2023 from: https://radar.brookes.ac.uk/radar/file/eebc292e-7141-464e-b54f-a66c261a9ddd/1/Goal%20striving%20reasons%20framework%20-%202019%20-%20Ehrlich.pdf

53. Are SMART goals dumb? (2021). Leadership IQ. Retrieved 2023 from: https://www.leadershipiq.com/blogs/leadershipiq/35353793-are-smart-goals-dumb

54. Csikszentmaihalyi, M. (1990). *Flow: The Psychology of Optimal Experience* (p. 3). New York, NY: Harper & Row.

55. Ehrlich, C (2019). *The goal-striving framework: Further evidence for its predictive power for subjective well-being on a sub-dimensional level and on an individual goal-striving reasons level as well as evidence for its theoretical difference to self-concordance*. Oxford, United Kingdom: Oxford Brooks University. Retrieved March 2023 from: https://radar.brookes.ac.uk/radar/file/eebc292e-7141-464e-b54f-a66c261a9ddd/1/Goal%20striving%20reasons%20framework%20-%202019%20-%20Ehrlich.pdf

Praise for The Leader's Suitcase

The Leader's Suitcase *uniquely blends Carolyn's considerable leadership experience with positive psychology concepts to offer insights for aspiring and experienced leaders. This very readable text is packed with practical applications and personal examples which bring theoretical concepts to life. The content is relatable, relevant and engaging and the organisation flows seamlessly throughout.*

This is not just a book to read and put down. Readers are challenged to reflect on their own responses and move 'from ideas to action' at the end of each chapter to develop their own leadership repertoire. While providing extensive ideas for individual growth, leadership teams would also find the contents invaluable for guiding collective professional learning.

This first 'packing cell' in The Leader's Suitcase *is a wonderful resource and I am sure other readers will also look forward to the gems promised in the remaining two books.*

Dr Julie Mackey - Associate Professor University of Canterbury

I love how it weaves research and Carolyn's own experience and wisdom about leadership into highly practical strategies that move one into a thriving stance.

Sarah Martin - Principal Stonefields School

The Leader's Suitcase - Setting Yourself Up for Success *provides clever and practical advice essential for any leader or someone looking to get into a leadership role. Packed with numerous thought-provoking exercises and personal stories, Carolyn takes us on a journey that will not only help us to develop our self-awareness as leaders but is also guaranteed to move us from survival mode to thriving as leaders of our organisations.*

A must-read for anyone looking to equip themselves with the tools and strategies for effective leadership.

Neil Heyward - Principal Riccarton High School

Carolyn Stuart helps to demystify the journey for leaders - whatever stage they are at in their leadership. So often, as leaders, we wish we had more of a roadmap to help us to become the leaders we aspire to be - this is the roadmap that leads us closer to this aspiration. It is both authentic and pragmatic in its approach and incredibly thought-provoking. The standout line for me is: "We may possess a natural inclination towards leadership, but it is the work we do on ourselves, especially in the area of response management, that makes us the leader we aspire to be." The Leader's Suitcase *makes us feel, as leaders, that aspirational leadership is something we can attain and it shows the 'why', the 'how' and the 'what' in equal measures!*

Joanne Orr - Across-School Lead

Carolyn has created the perfect mix of research, personal stories, diagrams and strategies to engage us all, whatever stage of your leadership story you're in. This book will challenge you, then provide strategies to guide you through your next steps. Of special note is the focus on positive psychology. I'll certainly be keeping this book on hand to refer back to, for dealing with difficult situations and for reviewing my purpose and vision.

Karen Stewart - Former Principal Rangiora High School

I have read many books on the topic of leadership. Common themes and methodologies of leadership formation underpin many of them. Almost all have had a slight hint of salesmanship, as I suppose the allure of monetising one's leadership gift is ever-present.

Not this book it would seem.

In a refreshingly matter-of-fact way, the author leans on her hard-won experience as an educationalist and draws from well-researched published works to weave a narrative that builds a simple but sophisticated framework of leadership understanding for the reader. One cannot help but be drawn into her suitcase metaphor and before you know it, you have begun to imagine your own bespoke leadership suitcase and how it will be used in an ever-complex leader/follower world.

A refreshing read, and a book that will surely be in the reference section for many a leadership institution in our brave new world.

Dynes McConnell - Women's Health Surgeon

The Leader's Suitcase *is my 'go-to' leadership book. I love the balance of key ideas, stories and practical tools.* The Leader's Suitcase *provides a guide not just for our professional lives, but also for shaping our personal lives. If you are looking to move beyond surviving to thriving, then this book is for you.*

Dr Judy Bruce - Education Consultant and Researcher

In our day-to-day lives as leaders in education and industry, we are often so busy moving from one crisis to another that we lose sight of the motivations of our actions and the values that underpin these. Carolyn's work offers us an insight into ourselves as leaders, welcoming us on a journey of exploration to reflect on who we are as leaders and who we want to be as leaders. Filled with practical, reflective and insightful questions, as well as personal examples, this text is step one in a journey empowering you to seek a greater understanding of yourself, to enable you to thrive in your role. I found myself beginning to better understand how I react and act within my leadership role and wondering what if…? I have so enjoyed the book I am already re-reading it!

Are you ready to pack your kete as a leader, by discovering your strengths and values?

Lucy Tomlinson - Deputy Principal Pakuranga College

As I read The Leader's Suitcase *I found I kept nodding and saying "Yes." The content is relatable and readable. I loved the quotes at the start of each chapter and the whakataukī at the start of the book "Mā te huruhuru ka rere to manu. Adorn the bird with feathers so that it may soar." A really enjoyable read.*

Andrew Murray - Principal St Mary's College, Wellington

About the Author

Carolyn is an experienced leader who has held senior roles in education, business and government. She equips leaders with tools and strategies to successfully set themselves, the people they lead, and their organisations up for success.

Using a strengths-based approach and other tools from the field of positive psychology she turns today's leaders into tomorrow's positive deviants. Carolyn equips organisations to foster positive and inclusive cultures while empowering leaders to realise their vision and to become the person those around them need them to be.

www.ingramcontent.com/pod-product-compliance
Lightning Source LLC
Chambersburg PA
CBHW041217130526
44590CB00062BA/4269